Jill's Story

Between Two Worlds

Dedication

This book is dedicated to my beloved children,
Matthew, Stephen and Katherine, and grand children,
Reese, Savanna, Alexander, Erik, Rebecca, Benjamin, and Anja.

It was written as a way to connect the land I came from and the
country I love and have called home for nearly sixty years.

Cover design: Image painting, graphic design, and typesetting by © J. Jurado, Reproduction partial or in total prohibited.
Manuscript coaching, interior design, and publishing: Sarah White, First Person Productions, www.firstpersonprod.com
Editor: Marg Sumner

Images are from the collection of the Griffiths and Hussey families.

Printed in the United States.

Jay Jurado, photographer, with Luci and me in 2017

Jill's Story

Between Two Worlds

Contents

Preface

For the past year or so, I have spent as much time as possible writing and rewriting this book. It has brought up many memories of experiences, people, and events I'd thought forgotten.

I have written these words to the best of my ability—please forgive any imperfections. My apologies if I have written too much, or too little, and if I have not managed to be entirely accurate. Even if I have not mentioned everyone in these pages, you have doubtless been in my thoughts as I look back over the years. I feel sadness for losing those who are no longer here.

This book has been a labor of love, dedicated to my beloved family—ten Americans born, so far—as a consequence of my decision to visit the United States in 1961, and to not return to Australia.

Chapter 1

I believe that luck has played a large role in my life, despite life's many challenges and occasional setbacks.

I was lucky to have been born at all! Three times my father almost died in the First World War, once in Sierra Leone from blackwater fever in 1915, a second time from a bullet wound in Basra, Mesopotamia (now Iraq), and a third time when he was severely injured in the trenches of the Western Front in France from an incoming shell. On each occasion he was repatriated to England to recover before being sent back into the war. If Dad had not survived that terrible war, I would not have been born some twenty years later.

My parents met at a riverboat dance on the River Torrens in Adelaide, the capital of South Australia, one summer night in 1930. My handsome father, Theodore Ralph Houghton Griffiths, an Englishman born in colonial India, twenty-two years older than my mother, had lived an adventurous life of privilege. My mother, beautiful, unsophisticated, Vera Ellen Charlotte Justice, had never traveled more than thirty miles from her birthplace and left school at the end of eighth grade. Despite these differences, they were attracted to each other and married in 1931. Their relationship was a caring and mutually respectful one, despite many loud and passionate arguments throughout their married life.

When I was about ten months old, my mother was stricken with rheumatic fever. She was admitted to a medical facility and confined to complete bed rest for six months to avoid the possibility of serious side effects, which in those pre-antibiotic days often complicated this illness. My father felt unable to care for his three small children, so he arranged for each of us to be placed in the care of others. I was admitted to an orphanage that provided shelter not only for orphans, but also for children who lacked a parent to care for them.

Apparently, when my father left me there, my screams were so intense that my father could hear me more than a block away. When he called later to make arrangements to visit me, the staff told him that I had screamed uncontrollably for a long time after he left. It would be best for all concerned, they said, if he did not return, and so he did not. Thus, I was alone and separated from all that I had known up until that time for the next six months.

When my mother came to retrieve me, she found me huddled in a corner of my cot, a withdrawn, unresponsive baby. In later years Mummy told me she was afraid that she was never going to be able to get me back. She related how she devoted all her energy to drawing me out, but I remained listless and disinterested in my surroundings for a long time. Eventually, however, her efforts were rewarded—I came back! I have always felt grateful to my mother for having saved me, for I know I so easily could have been lost forever. This is another example of my luck prevailing against heavy odds. My experience in the orphanage brings to mind what I learned in the early 1960s as a pediatric nurse of the work of René Spitz, who studied on children in orphanages and the importance of physical contact for a child's normal emotional development.

Growing up, our lives revolved around the sea. It was our perpetual playground. One day, told to stay on the beach while my mother waded into the water to refresh herself from the excessive heat of the day, I followed her on my two-year-old legs and was quickly out of my depth. Responding to cries of alarm from people around her, my mother turned in time to see me going under—by the time she got to me for at least the third time! Although I don't remember this, the knowledge of its occurance has never deterred me from my intimate relationship with the sea.

One of my first memories, at about four years old, is of standing with my mother outside our home while she chatted with a friend. I was dressed in a brown and white checked dress, with a brown ribbon in my curly brown hair. I did not like it. I wanted a brightly colored ribbon, perhaps red, and I didn't like my brown dress either. So while Mummy talked with her friend, I squeezed my all-brown self behind her, feeling embarrassed by my appearance, hoping to escape notice.

As a child I struggled with sensations I didn't understand: seeing fire when I closed my eyes or my tongue feeling coarse and thick. I dreaded these sensations, which would occur without warning and which persisted for what seemed like years, despite my efforts to rid myself of them. I remember Dad unsuccessfully trying to reassure me by explaining there was no fire. I don't think I ever told him about my distressing tongue problem. Eventually, these disturbing sensations disappeared, but in retrospect, I realize that I was a nervous and oversensitive child with no one available to me to help me overcome my anxieties.

Perhaps I intuitively found a way to soothe myself. I recall being content for many hours as a child, stirring and mixing the wet earth in my front "garden" (yard) into muddy piles. I liked the mud squelching through my fingers and between my searching toes. I liked forming the warm,smooth mixture into different shapes, then plunging my fingers into it, and shaping it all over again. I was confident in the knowledge that no matter how much mud covered my clothes, my mother wouldn't scold me. I read recently of psychotherapists helping some of their stressed clients achieve release of their tensions by playing in therapeutic sand pits. It seems this could be based on the same principle that I had found to calm myself by playing in the mud.

A happy early memory is of holding my mother's hand as my brother and sister and I wound our way down the cliff face below our home. David and Mary and I loved swimming in the sea and burying our salt-covered bodies in the golden sands of Seacliff Beach. We also loved exploring sea life in the nearby rock pools of Kingston Park, searching for crabs, sea anemones, sea stars, and barnacles to put in our buckets before returning them to the seawater, then collecting the prettiest empty seashells we could find to take home. My brother, four years older than I, taught me numbers in the wet sand, "up to twenty," and told me "just follow the rule through thirty and forty" and so on.

When I was not quite six years old, I started my first two years of school at Hopetown, a private school in Brighton, a mile or so from my home. Thanks to my brother, I was already skilled in what we called "mental arithmetic" and, having found David's history books, already able to read. Hopetown School was run by two sisters, the Misses Fleming, who were mean, unkind women. One day, one of them rushed past me to where my sister had her head under the raised lid of her desk. I turned around in time to see Miss Fleming slam the lid on my sister's unsuspecting head. Horrified, I called out, "If you do that again, I'll call the police." From the back of the room came the voice of Gerrick, otherwise known as Dutchy, my brother's best friend. "And she will, too." When I was eight years old, Mary and I started at a new school, St. Peter's Girls' School, in Adelaide.

I remember the day I taught myself to swim. I was floating on my stomach, face down in the sea, when I decided to move one arm forward, then the other. I suddenly realized that without my customary foot on the sand below, I was not sinking, but was moving slightly forward. So I began kicking both

My mother: Vera Ellen Charlotte Justice Griffiths

My father: Theodore Ralph Houghton Griffiths

legs vigorously to continue my progress and, in order to breathe, I lifted my head out of the water—I was swimming! In ensuing years, I improved my style and eventually became a strong swimmer of what was then known as the Australian crawl.

When I think of those days, I am transported back to the salty smell and taste of the sea, the harsh cries of the swooping gulls, the gritty sand that clung to our bodies, the magic of the sun glistening on the blues, greens, and dark purples of the sea, and our dogs running along with us in and out of the waves. I especially recall one hot summer day. I was swimming alone when I found myself surrounded by a pod of playful dolphins. I felt no fear. Indeed, I was exhilarated by their proximity as they skimmed by me, their bodies flashing in the sun as they leaped out of the water, their mouths open, seeming to smile at me. I was thrilled to look into the eyes of those beautiful creatures for the few moments they were with me, for all too soon they continued their journey into the deeper sea.

Outside the window of my childhood bedroom stood a huge, tall pine tree, its branches spreading across much of the side of our house. On very hot summer days it was a sanctuary from the merciless Australian sun. On cold, wet winter nights, as the wind came blowing off the sea, I loved the sound of its branches beating against the window as I snuggled into my blankets. When I was only five years old, I learned to climb this beautiful tree, its many branches offering firm footholds for my searching feet. I became increasingly adept and confident in my climbing, eventually advancing to the upper branches. There I would nestle in a branch in a corner of its gnarled trunk, daydreaming of things of interest in my small and innocent world as I looked over the fields and occasional houses on the edge of the village where I lived with my parents and older brother and sister.

I often did this, not only because I enjoyed working my way up through its twisted branches, but because it was my secret hiding place, where I could survey everything around me without being observed myself. Neighbors walking by and chatting with each other, my friends laughing and squabbling as they ran by, or every so often a dog sniffing and peeing on its way to the beach below: all unaware of my avid interest in their interactions. As I grew a little older, maybe seven or eight years old, at which time I seemed frequently to be in trouble, in certain emergency situations I would scramble up the tree and hide in its topmost branches. From there I watched my father searching for me so he could give me a thrashing for my latest transgression. On the rare occasions that he caught me, he never really hurt me, even as the switch swiped my cotton shorts. I would cry, "I didn't do it," and he would respond,

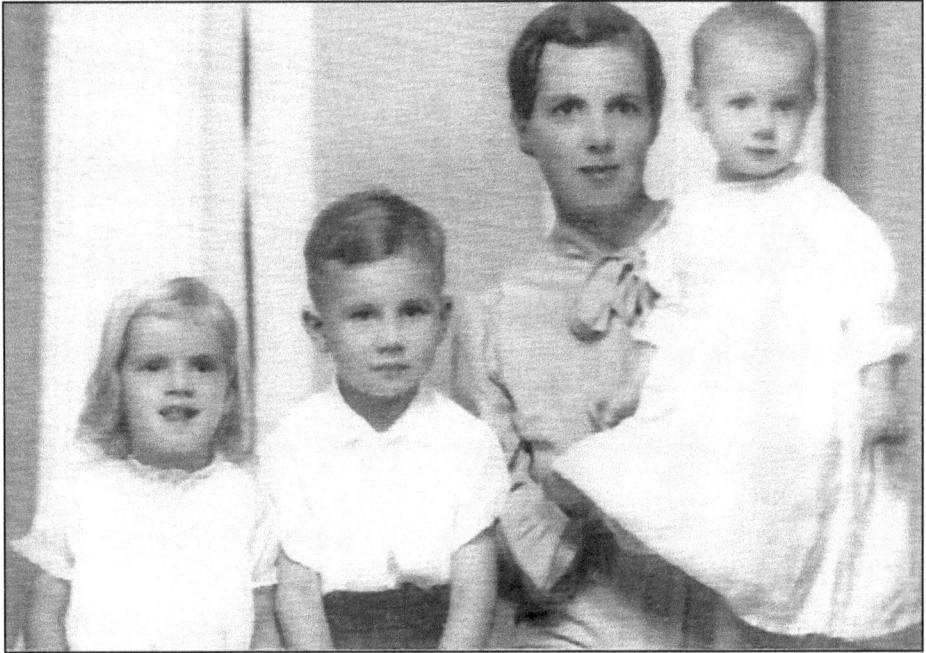

The Griffiths siblings, 1936: Mary, David, Mother "Mummy", Jillian

"Well, this is for the times you *did* do it, and I didn't catch you." This didn't seem fair to me—to be punished for past ingenuity in avoiding capture, despite my declared innocence, because I hadn't been fast enough to escape his long arms and legs. In retrospect, I have wondered if he knew where I was all the time, and as I sat up there chuckling to myself that I had outsmarted him, perhaps he preferred to not catch me and thus avoid all the fuss that would result once he did!

My father, tall, ex-soldier, ex-boxer, ex-rugby player, in many ways considered a "man's man," had a tender heart, and I greatly admired him, even as a child. Though I was a girl, I sensed he recognized some of himself in me, his youngest child; certainly I was what was known as a tomboy. On one particular occasion, he took me to a boxing match, anticipating an exciting occasion and perhaps believing that I would share his enthusiasm.

It probably started out well. I remember enjoying being with Dad, having him all to myself, with no brother or sister calling for his attention. I remember the noisy crowd elbowing its way around us as we searched for a good seat. Dad's imposing bearing seemed to part the way for us, and we found a ringside seat. This soon turned out to be a mistake. I remember two big beefy men sitting across from each other in the ring, bodies tensed, eyes staring into space as they awaited the bell. Dad pointed out some differences between them and why he thought one had "the edge" and probably would win. No doubt I was absorbing his enthusiasm, and my excitement matched his and the growing energy of the crowd around me.

Then the bell rang, and as the crowd roared, the two men jumped into the center of the ring and began circling each other. I don't remember seeing or hearing any women there, but I suppose there were some. I almost certainly was the only child—and at ringside no less! At first I was fascinated, watching the circling feet almost at my eye level and seeing the sweat pouring down the men's muscled backs and arms. Those jabbing arms swinging their gloved hands began landing punches on each other, here on the chest, there on the side of the head, there on the jaw, and again on the chest. Dad was shouting as loud as everyone around and behind us. I'm pretty sure I wasn't shouting, for I remember beginning to feel upset and having a sick feeling as I saw and heard those blows landing on flesh. Then one of those gloves landed full force on the other's nose, and suddenly blood was spurting everywhere.

I don't know what happened next because right after the blood started to flow, I fainted dead away. My only memory after that of my fun day with Dad was coming to as he carried me out to his car. I regretted spoiling my Dad's day, but from that day to this, I have maintained an abiding distaste for the so-called sport of boxing.

Shortly after the United States entered World War II, probably about early 1942, American soldiers set up camp in the sand hills along the shoreline where David, Mary, and I often played. We were fascinated by their strange accents and their generously shared supply of chewing gum, so we spent a good deal of time hanging around them. Sometimes they would let us look down the scopes of their rifles and would entertain us with stories of where they came from in America. Just before Christmas, "Sarge," whom I particularly liked because of his humorous adventure tales, solemnly told me that if I wanted Santa Claus ("You mean Father Christmas." "Oh yeah, Father Christmas") to leave me lots of presents, I must hang up a pillow case at the end of my bed on Christmas Eve. This I faithfully did. My parents must have had to scurry around to fill it up, as we kids usually only got one or two modest presents. I remember some peaches, figs, apricots, and nectarines filled my Christmas stocking that year: same as the fruit on the trees in our yard.

I sometimes took home stray animals that I insisted had followed me, but more often than not, I had lured them, hoping my parents would allow them to live with us. Once I found a baby penguin on the beach, which must have been separated from its parent as the pod traversed the seas south of Kangaroo Island. Despite my pleadings, my parents insisted I return it to where I had found it; they really had no choice. I can still see this little creature walking across our kitchen table as I begged for it to stay with us. When I learned that St. Francis of Assisi was the patron saint of all animals, I felt a kinship with him that the nuns at my school were unable to arouse in me for any other saints!

It was my habit, when I was about eight years old, to walk about half a mile every day to greet my father on his return home from work. Although he was 50 years older than I, in my young eyes, he was very tall, very strong, and very handsome. In those days he always rode his bicycle to and from work in Adelaide, a distance of about 14 miles each way. I vividly remember one day in particular. As Dad saw me waiting for him, he got off his bike and walked smiling toward me. "Guess what, Jilly? I have a surprise for you!"

What could this be? As the smile on my father's face broadened, my searching eyes caught a glimpse of a tiny ginger head with big brown eyes peeping out from the lower pocket of his coat. "Dad! A puppy!" "Yes," he replied, as his big hands lifted this tiny, curly-haired, squirming creature, and placed it in my eager hands. I was instantly in love with the sixth member of our family, Rusty. Of course, he was the family dog, but to me, he was "my dog." Together, we explored the hills, rocks, tide pools, and caves along the coastline south of Seacliff. I could tell him my thoughts and troubles, and he would listen attentively, offering me comfort as the friend who loved me without question or criticism. I drew comfort from his devotion, for as young as I was, I was sometimes troubled by the people in my small world, hearing my parents' intense arguments, or at odds with my brother or my sister, or sometimes with one of my friends.

One day, Rusty returned from one of his habitual lone explorations, exhausted, pulling himself painfully up our driveway with his back leg dragging behind him. My parents speculated that he must have been hit by the local train, which ran about a half-mile from our house. We were all very upset. I thought Rusty was going to die. But even without the benefit of veterinary attention, something rarely sought in those days, he slowly recovered and, except for a pronounced limp, he became his old self again.

We had our only bath once a week in "the tub," borrowed from the laundry room for the occasion. In winter this was always in front of the fireplace, our only source of heat. As the youngest child, my turn for this came last, so

The Griffiths family circa 1944: David, Dad, Mary, Jill, Mummy

not only was the water almost cold, but it probably wasn't particularly clean, although I don't recall this ever bothering me.

About half a mile down from Seacliff Beach was Kingston Park, easily identified by two pine trees, fondly known by all as the Twin Sisters, which towered over the park. There, for a few weeks every summer we had play-mates who were camped in Kingston Park, the children of Roma, or Gypsies, who mysteriously arrived from and departed to parts unknown. While they were there, their families welcomed us to share their campfire and their food. I still recall the warm soup and freshly baked bread. These friends were a lot of fun and, needless to say, quite unique to us compared with our regular playmates. They were different in many ways: their skin was much darker than ours, and their clothes were a lot more colorful than what we wore. They also had a challenging attitude to the world that we found thrilling, and in which we were eager to participate. I recall showing off for them by climbing a nearby water tower, going up countless steps to the top, as a way to prove I was not just the skinny younger sister of my strong and self-assured brother. On looking down in triumph at the watching faces below, one of them yelled, "O.K., prove that you really got there! Go over into the inside and wet your body in the water!" This I immediately did, and so anxious was I to prove myself that as I lowered myself into the water, I felt no fear. As I climbed back over the top of the tank to show them my wet body, I felt victorious.

My childhood memories are of happy and full days. At dusk we were drawn home not only by hunger, but because it was essential we be there in time to turn on the "wireless" (radio) to listen to our favorite show, "The Lawsons," about the lives of a family who lived in the "bush" (the Australian outback).

One of my first friends was the only child of a local fisherman. Lorraine and her parents lived in a small shack behind the sand dunes leading down to the beach. Her father, whom I always addressed politely as Mr. Norman, would row his small boat out to sea in the predawn darkness. Many days Lorraine and I would be waiting on the beach midmorning for his return. First, we would see a speck on the horizon, which gradually resolved into the sight of Mr. Norman's straining muscles pulling on his oars. I remember being in awe of his courage in rowing way out to sea, all by himself, sometimes in really rough weather, far out to where we knew there were Great White sharks and other large and frightening sea creatures. As Mr. Norman pulled his boat up onto the sand, we waited excitedly to see how many fish he had caught. Sometimes I would be holding silver coins in my hand ready to select and pay for fish for my family's evening meal. In my mind's eye, I can still see us, two skinny little girls in our shapeless swimsuits, the sun beating down on our sandy, salty bodies, admiring the multitude of silvery, glistening fish in the large bucket in the bottom of his boat, as I carefully made my selection. I eventually lost contact with Lorraine. One day she and her parents were there, and then without warning they were gone. Her family's shack was later torn down, replaced with a parking lot for the local Brighton and Seacliff Yacht Club, where I later participated in competitive sailing races.

Our red brick home on Marine Parade was set slightly back on the cliff overlooking the sea. During the day one could hear the sounds from the beach below, the cries of the gulls, the barking of dogs, and in the warmer months of the year, the shouts and cries of people. On hot summer nights we would get some relief from the heat by pulling our beds onto the verandah that ran across the front of the house. I am not sure how much cooler it actually was—perhaps an occasional sea breeze would reach us—but it was a lot more fun than sleeping in our bedrooms. It meant we could look at the stars, hear all kinds of night sounds ordinarily not heard, and especially if we had one or two friends over, we could talk for hours before finally drifting off to sleep. Sometimes, when it was unbearably hot, we would carry our bedding down to the beach, along with our little portable, windup record player, and after singing along with our favorite tunes, we would fall asleep to the sound of the sea lapping close to where we lay on our blankets.

Two sides of our house were enclosed by high hedges, in the middle of which was a small gate leading into our front lawn and garden. Mummy loved to garden, and most days could be seen sheltering under a large sunhat working in the dirt, or clipping back bushes, or cutting flowers for our living room. The shrubs and flowerbeds were colorful, especially the red hibiscus bush at one end of the front garden, which attracted butterflies and birds of every variety. My mother's love of gardening nurtured a similar love of gardening and nature in me.

Our lifestyle was simple in those days—no car, no phone, no indoor toilet, no dishwasher, no washing machine, no television, no air conditioning. And despite extremely hot summers, no refrigerator, not even an ice box—we had a "cool safe." What was a cool safe? A small wire-mesh-sided container, with interior shelves on which to place certain foods, such as milk, eggs, and butter so they didn't spoil in the heat. Dish towels were placed over the safe, and these towels had to be kept wet at all times to keep the interior as cool as possible throughout the summer. Having just a cool safe required daily shopping in the village for perishable food. Sometimes it also required my mother to send me to Deere's Dairy, some half a mile from our home, with a "billy can" (pail) to get extra milk. I would swing the milk-filled can by its handle round and round my head, testing my skills against centrifugal force, which occasionally resulted in most of the milk flying out of the can, much to Mummy's displeasure on my arrival home. I'm not sure why I was the person invariably sent to the dairy, given this possible outcome—perhaps as the youngest I was the only one around when she needed an emergency supply. Who knows?

Our kitchen is easily recreated in my mind: the warmest room in the house in the long, wet, cold winters, and the hottest room in the house in the long, hot summers. An electric stove on one side, the large kitchen table in the middle, with a window behind it looking out onto our many fruit trees, and the cool safe on the other side of the room.

I enjoyed my mother's plain cooking, serving us up many different cuts of meat, mostly lamb, and on special days, brains, liver, or tripe (cow intestines), with a wide variety of vegetables, including parsnips, Brussels sprouts, turnips, and beets. To this day I prefer vegetables to any other foods, including fruits and sweets. I can still visualize my mother's hands, cracked from a life of hard work without the benefit of modern conveniences, those cracks stained with the juice of the beets I loved so much. Sometimes she baked, my favorite being her bread and butter pudding. Mmmm!

Then there were the occasions when she baked scones! They were good if you ate them still warm from the oven and smothered in butter, or with jam and cream. But once they lost their warmth, they turned into rock hard, teeth-resistant round balls, and were left to die neglected on the plate! I have no idea why this was so. Perhaps she didn't use yeast. Whatever the reason, scones were not her forte. And then there was the toast! As we didn't own a toaster, Mummy would put slices of bread on a tray and place the tray under the oven broiler. Without fail, our first awareness of the toast was smoke escaping from the oven, followed by the scraping of the burnt bread, and the remains placed in front of us.

Other than the occasional smell of burning toast, the kitchen always seemed to smell good, even if Mummy wasn't there cooking us a meal. In summer, we would pick the fruit from our trees: figs, apricots, nectarines, and peaches, and Mummy would make jam from the apricots and figs. Only I liked the fig jam, so through the following autumn and winter I happily emptied all the jars of fig jam, spread lavishly on thickly buttered, soft white bread—fat, sweet slices of heaven!

Dad often sat at one end of the kitchen table to eat his lunch, and sometimes I would join him. These were opportunities for me to hear some of his stories of growing up in India and of his experiences after being sent to boarding school in England at age seven or eight. Dad had been reared in the upper class of colonial India, cared for by servants, and with what seems to have been limited physical or emotional contact with his mother and father. Consequently, although I experienced him as a kind and caring father, he was a typical Englishman, who maintained a "stiff upper lip," and who did not demonstrate or verbalize his emotions. One of my special memories of Dad was the day we sat together at the kitchen table and, showing unaccustomed emotion, he told me that he loved me. This was the only time he ever verbalized his love for me, although I had always felt it. It is a memory I have always cherished.

Our dog Rusty loved this room where his family most often gathered. However, there was a hard and fast rule for Rusty that he never violated: he was not allowed in the kitchen. But smart boy that he was, he managed to slightly push the boundaries. He would lie in the entrance, with only his front legs partially extended into the kitchen, as he listened to our interactions. His human family honored and never challenged Rusty's bending of the rules. It was his favorite place to be, just as it was mine!

In the long hot summers, we spent every day swimming in the sea's welcoming coolness. There were not infrequent times when we kids became aware of the presence of sharks, and we all knew the story of the famous Olympic swimmer, whose name I no longer recall, who died an awful death after diving off the Brighton jetty into the mouth of a shark. One of our favorite diving places was at the far end of that very same jetty! Occasionally we would see the fin of a shark cruising in the area. At these times, even the wildest of kids hung back a few minutes before going back to diving into the sea. One summer day we were all gathered at the jetty rails as a school of dolphins challenged a Grey Nurse shark, one of the most aggressive and feared of sharks. We don't know what the fight was over. Perhaps the shark had been trying to attack one of them. Dolphins have few teeth, unlike the hundreds of teeth of a shark, but each of these dolphins took turns, over and over, hitting the shark with their bodies, until we could see blood in the water. This battle went on for quite a few minutes until finally the shark retreated and swam away, to our resounding cheers.

Another favorite place where we all gathered was on a raft moored out from Seacliff Beach. Getting there required swimming out several hundred yards from the shore. My brother felt strongly against my doing this—I'm not sure why—and he pleaded with my mother to forbid my doing so. This she did not do, although I'm pretty sure I would have continued doing so even if she had. There were at least two occasions when David appeared to have had a good point. One occurred as I made my way to the raft. As I was only about ten years old, I wasn't a strong swimmer and I needed to stop once or twice to float and rest. This day, as I floated, I felt the presence of something large pass close beneath me. For a split second I froze in terror, then I swam faster than I had ever swum before, reaching the raft extremely shaken. I am glad that I did not experience anything worse than a healthy dose of fear on that long ago summer day.

On the other occasion, the raft had been crowded with a large number of kids, but as the sun approached the horizon, they began to leave. Eventually I was the only one remaining. I liked that time of day and enjoyed being alone with time to daydream. I must have briefly dozed off, for when I awoke, I became aware that it was much later. Looking to the shore I realized that the tide was way in, and the beach was much farther away than I wanted it to be! As I prepared to dive, I looked into the darkening water in time to see a fin pass right in front of the raft. After several minutes of shouting and frantically waving to people on the shore, I finally got the attention of some members of the Seacliff Life Saving Club, of which my brother was a member.

Some minutes later, I saw someone rowing one of their boats out to me. As it drew alongside the raft, I hastily clambered into the boat, explaining the reason for my dilemma to the amused lifesaver, who knew I was David's sister.

Some days I would ride my one-speed bike, which had no brakes, straight down the precipitously steep Wheatland Street to the Esplanade below, taking a sharp right turn at the corner to slow myself as I continued on the slight uphill. Other days I rode my scooter around the village looking for my friends. More often than not I was barefoot and, combined with perpetually running across hot sand or pushing my scooter with my foot over hot roads, my feet had become as hard as leather and mostly impervious to hot surfaces.

One particular day, I rode my scooter down Wheatland Street and crossed the Esplanade to the beach next to the Seacliff Life Saving Club, where some of us often hung out, swimming, building sand castles, and playing hide-and-seek in the nearby sand hills. The day had been no different from any other, except that when it came time for us to leave, I found the wheel had come off my scooter. I told my impatient friends to go ahead without me, planning to catch up with them once I fixed my scooter, as the wheel had fallen off before and I knew how to fix it. After they left, a man I had noticed watching us from the lookout above came down the stairs to where I had begun working on my scooter. "Do you need some help? I can help you fix that," he said. "That's all right, I can do it," I politely replied, recognizing him as my friend Jimmy's dad. "Here, give it to me, I can fix it in a jiffy. Just bring it up here," he said, taking it from me and carrying it into the open door of one of the Life Saving Club's equipment rooms. I hesitantly followed, and stood awkwardly just inside the doorway. "Come over here and help me hold it upright," he urged me. I moved slowly into the semidarkness and held the front of the scooter. As I did so, he moved closer to me and put his arm round my waist. "Let's just close the door, and I'll turn on the light so I can see what I am doing better." As he said this, he reached out and partially closed the door. For a moment I stood immobilized, with a strong sense of unease. It flashed through my mind that this was Jimmy's dad and I didn't want to offend him, but a split second later my intuition urged me to get away from him. I made some sort of comment about needing to go as I snatched up my scooter and wheel, and backed out into the sunlight. He did not follow as I ran up the stairs to the street above.

I must have told my parents about this, because shortly after the incident, a policewoman came to my home and asked if she could talk with me. I remember liking and trusting her, and for what must have been at least an hour, she asked me many questions. I later learned that shortly after I spoke with the policewoman, Jimmy's dad had been sent to prison. Apparently, the police had been aware that he had been sexually molesting children, but until I had recounted my story from that hot summer day and, most important, being able to identify him, they had been unable to get sufficient evidence to charge him. For a long time, I felt guilty about having been the cause of Jimmy's dad going to prison. Typically, no one seemed to realize my need for an explanation nor the distress I felt on Jimmy's behalf. Eventually, the incident faded from my awareness, although I don't think Jimmy continued to be one of my playmates.

David, Mary, and I often played on the railroad tracks a half-mile or so from our home. One of our favorite tricks was to put a coin on the tracks, then put our ears onto the rail and listen for the train as it approached the bend farther up the track. After it had passed us, we'd check to see how much the coin had flattened under the train's wheels. Because we spent so much time around the tracks, sometimes the engine driver would invite us into the cabin so we could watch him stoke the steam engine's fire with coal as the train sped down the tracks. Some of that coal we would find along the tracks and take home to add to the fire in our living room. Other times, the men checking the tracks would let all three of us climb aboard their little wooden machines and ride along with them, even occasionally allowing us to push the lever that operated the machine.

At four years older than I, David enjoyed playing rough games such as cowboys and Indians or gang warfare. Mary and I were encouraged, as girls, to play quiet games, such as "house" with our dolls. I didn't like playing dolls and I spent as much time as possible playing with my brother and his friends. One of David's interests that involved me was jujitsu. He promised to teach me some of his amazing new skills if I let him practice them on me. I don't think I ever learned anything other than what some of the moves were called during these interactions. However, I definitely remember the day he threw me over his shoulder and I landed with a thud on the hard ground. Fortunately, I wasn't hurt, but I did not appreciate his laughter as I left the scene of my humiliation, never to return.

David and I would make "bitzers" (go-carts) from old wooden boxes and discarded wheels. With some of his buddies, we would race them as fast as possible down the nearby cliffs into the gully below. This was exciting and dangerous as we competed with each other, the idea being to reach maximum velocity so the bitzers would continue as far as possible up the side of the opposite cliff. This all ended for me when one day "Milky" Butler demanded that David not let his "skinny sister" accompany them any more. This was doubly hurtful to me, as I secretly had a crush on Milky up until that moment.

One of David's friends was Jim Hardy, the youngest of four children who lived with their widowed, wealthy, and socially prominent mother in a much larger and fancier home than ours across the street. David and Jim had an on-and-off-again friendship. In one of their getting-along periods, they decided they would build a raft, which they planned to paddle out to sea, with high hopes for the possibilities of their creation. The completed raft had metal drums strapped to the underside to make it "stronger and float higher," and looked impressive to us. Mary and I, and a couple of other friends helped David and Jim drag it into the water, using our combined strength to push it from the shore into the deeper water. Everything was looking good as David gave it a mighty push. But even as it slowly moved over the smooth sea, it began to sink, and soon it was a water-logged mess! So ended David's boat-building interest, although a few years later Jim became a skilled builder of small sailing boats.

When Rusty was about four years old, we got a second dog, Trixie, a small wire-haired terrier, who gave birth to a litter of pups sired by Rusty. Trixie and one of her pups, a long-legged, small-bodied white dog my brother named Dane, in the erroneous belief he was destined to be a much larger dog. Trixie and Dane would also become beloved friends of mine. Trixie and I shared many adventures. She certainly earned her name as I taught her countless clever tricks, including how to climb a ladder onto our hedges and to walk along them from one end to the other, her only reward being my shouts of praise! She was a happy and smart creature.

As Rusty began to slow down, his ginger coat noticeably began to turn white, especially around his mouth and eyes. Somehow, it had never really occurred to me that he would not always be with me. One day, while standing with my mother in our living room, looking out the window into the front garden, I saw my father and Toby, the local policeman, whom we thought of as a friend, walk by. Toby was holding Rusty, with all four of Rusty's legs sticking out in front of him. I turned to my mother, puzzled, and asked, "Why is Toby carrying Rusty? Where are they going?" Barely were the words out of my mouth when I heard the crack of a rifle shot. I instantly realized what must have happened and screamed. My beautiful, trusting, loving friend was gone! As if yesterday, I recall the awful pain I felt.

I have no recollection of what my parents told me, either before or after this terrible moment. I'm pretty sure they didn't tell me anything, perhaps in the misguided assumption that it was better not to discuss it. To this day

Jill and Dane, 1950

I have no idea why he was killed. Was he infirm in his advancing age? Was this considered a kindness to release him from some form of pain or suffering? Whatever the reason, I know that if they had tried to prepare me for that awful day and had offered me some comforting words, it would have helped me manage my desperate emotional pain. But for my family, and I think for the general society of the day, it was rare to recognize or understand emotional and psychological trauma. The attitude seemed to be "just get on with it," whatever "it" was, and don't complain.

When I was about twelve, as I played in my backyard, I became aware of an ambulance coming down our street—an unusual sight that I watched with interest. But then it slowed down, stopped, and backed up from the road to the fence at the end of our driveway. Suddenly, I felt my stomach lurch! I knew Mummy was not feeling well, but what could this mean? Young as I was, I knew the ambulance was not meant for my brother or my sister or my father; it was meant for her! At first I stood there, not knowing what to do, my thoughts racing, as I watched two men step out of the ambulance, walk around and open the back doors of the vehicle, and pull out a stretcher.

Then I was running toward the front door, thinking to see my mother. But my father appeared, blocked my way, and said, "wait Jill." I did as I was told, but I still recall the chill of fear going through my body. Why have they come for Mummy? What could be so wrong that they were going to put her on a stretcher? Where were they going to take her? I felt weak and frightened, while a rising tide of panic flooded my body as I waited near the front door. I had no awareness of anyone else around me other than my father standing beside me. I suppose David and Mary were there, but I have no memory of their presence.

Then the two men came out, holding each end of the stretcher, and there was my mother, eyes closed, seemingly unaware of her surroundings. I remember saying "Mummy," but her eyes didn't open. The men kept walking to the back of the ambulance, and slid the stretcher carefully inside. The picture in my mind of that moment is of the doors closing behind her, and then the ambulance moving out onto the road. Perhaps there was a lot of activity during those last few minutes, but I have no recollection of anything except seeing those doors close and watching the ambulance driving away up the street. I felt an emptiness inside me as it slowly disappeared from view. I did not see my mother again for several months as she recovered from this, her second bout of rheumatic fever.

Over those months I missed her very much, even although I was living with one of her best friends, Renee, and Renee's male friend "Uncle" Owen, and her son, Ralph, and was being cared for lovingly and well. Auntie Renee had agreed to "take me in" to live with her until my mother recovered. Auntie Renee, tall, slender, always smartly dressed, her short gray hair immaculately styled, with her long red nails invariably holding a cigarette in a long and fancy holder, was the personification of sophistication to me. Her form-fitting clothes, like her hair, were immaculate, tailored suits and jackets trimmed with fur and slim, straight skirts. I was impressed by and somewhat in awe of my mother's friend, so unlike my mother.

Despite missing my mother, I enjoyed my new living situation. Every day after school I would catch the tram to Rundle Street, the center of Adelaide's business district. I loved the busy street, full of shops and offices and all kinds of interesting people. On reaching Auntie Renee's building, I would ride the slow-moving, clanging metal elevator up to her third-floor office. She would always have milk and cookies ready for me on a little side table next to a rocking chair. I would happily wait for her to finish her business, munching on my cookies and reading the daily newspaper until she was ready to leave for home. (*The News* was the first newspaper owned by Rupert Murdoch, who would become the internationally known and influential owner of many newspapers and other media.) Auntie Renee's home was fun, too, as her son Ralph, who was a year older than I, would already be home from school, and we would play outside until it was time for dinner. A highlight of my time with Auntie Renee was having my hair cut and styled by her hairdresser every month. Although my hair was naturally curly, I thought my professional haircut made me look very cool.

Perhaps it is the faulty memory of a child, but I don't remember anyone explaining the implications of Mummy's illness, or what progress she was making. I only occasionally saw my father. David and Mary lived in separate places—I have no idea where. With family friends? I don't know.

And then Mummy came home. She seemed none the worse for her illness, and we were all back living together in the red brick house near the sea. My mother was a beautiful, calm, and loving person, the best mother anyone could have, and I remember how comforted I was to have her back. Even as a child I recognized her beauty, with her large, dark brown, almost black eyes, olive skin, and long, smooth, auburn hair that she sometimes let me brush; how I wished my hair were like hers. And then one day she cut it off! I didn't like her new "bobbed" hairstyle at all, but I began playing with the long, silky hair, which she had caught with a rubber band. Then out of the blue I was struck with a brilliant idea. Now I too could have beautiful, flowing reddish brown hair. Pulling on one of my mother's favorite dresses—black with blue, yellow, and red flowers—a pair of her high heels, and a large sunhat from under which, fixed with pins, her auburn tresses flowed, I tottered down Marine Parade, all the way to the Esplanade below. As I paraded around the village, I did not for a moment suspect that the looks I was getting, of which I was well aware, were anything but admiring ones. Doubtless those who saw me must have been secretly chuckling at this serious, skinny little girl in her dress-up clothes. But what a great time I had! I have no idea if my mother ever knew of my little escapade. She never mentioned it.

David's best friend, Gerrick, always called Dutchy, emigrated with his family in 1946 to Australia from Holland at the end of the world war. Dutchy seemed incredibly handsome to my ten-year-old eyes—and probably was. Tall for his age, muscular, fair-haired, blue-eyed, and a natural born leader. He and David decided to form a gang, and it immediately was known as "Dutchy's Gang." My brother, as dark as Dutchy was fair, and as strong-willed as Dutchy, appeared to have no resentment at his friend being the leader. Why form a gang? We were all influenced in one way or another by the knowledge of the just-ended terrible war, and perhaps we thought conflicts must always be resolved by fighting. Belonging to the gang was considered serious business, and David and Dutchy built several semi-underground tunnels in the open paddocks around, that ended with a six-foot-deep dugout. This dark hole was the gang's "headquarters," where by the light of a candle five or six boys would regularly hold meetings and have highly secret discussions.

Bob and Joe Ransom lived about a half-mile away from us, and they formed a rival gang, known as Ransom's Gang. When the cry would go up "Ransom's are coming," there would be a great rush of Dutchy's gang to arm themselves with homemade tin swords and shields, which were stored as "armory" in a boarded-up hole in the paddock behind our house. What followed was much shouting and rock throwing, and an occasional scuffle between a couple of boys in the dirt. Occasionally, I was allowed to participate, and if David decided he needed an extra fighter besides me, Mary was persuaded to join in by my promising to play dolls with her at some future date. The only time I recall anyone actually getting hurt was the day my sister came running out the back gate and was hit on the head with a rock. She fell to the ground, temporarily dazed, after which she refused to participate in any further gang action.

As my skill and strength developed as a swimmer, and being of a competitive nature, I began to compete in local swim meets, many mornings catching an early train into Adelaide so I could swim at the Adelaide City Baths before school started. At one of these competitions, when I was twelve years old, I was approached by a well-dressed man, who offered me the opportunity of one year's free training with him. Apparently I wasn't interested, as I never followed up on his offer. I later learned the man was Harry Gallagher, the trainer of Olympian gold and silver medalist Dawn Fraser, Australia's greatest female swimmer! Formerly of Sydney, he had taken out a lease at the City Baths at the time I was swimming and competing there. He discovered Dawn at age thirteen, one year older than I, and when he began training her, her parents allowed her to move to Adelaide from Sydney to train at the City Baths. There is no way to know how it might have turned out if I had accepted his offer, but sometimes I allow myself to imagine. I was good. Could he have trained me to become as good as Dawn? Some years later, reading an interview with Harry Gallagher, I was interested to learn he had also taught himself to swim—in order to save himself from drowning!

One of my favorite activities was tennis. On many blazing hot days on hot tennis courts, I enjoyed sending my super-strong serve or slicing my backhand or forehand past my opponents. Sometimes I would play tennis with my father. I would send one of those shots to my father's backhand, knowing it would be a winner because he could not turn fast enough on his war-acquired "gammy" leg to reach and return it. I felt such a sense of power and strength to be so in control and so confident.

Mary was eighteen months older than I, but because of her retiring nature, we did not enjoy many of the same activities. At an early age she was diagnosed with Von Recklinhausen's Disease, a condition that resulted in many benign tumors developing in different parts of her body, which required her to undergo surgery from time to time to remove them. Relative to this, my parents tended to over-protect her, rarely allowing her to take risks and responsibility for her own wellbeing. Consequently, she lacked the self-confidence to live her life to the full. Although Mary and I loved each other, we grew in different directions as far as interests and friends. Regrettably, we were never close.

I grew to love our dog Dane with the same intensity I had felt for his father, Rusty. When I started my nursing training at age eighteen, I would only see Dane on my one day off a week. On one of those days, I came home expecting to find Dane greeting me as usual, but he was no longer there. My mother explained that he had been put down a few days earlier. My reaction was instantaneous and intense, and I spent my day off crying uncontrollably. Once again, my parents had not warned me, perhaps in the erroneous belief that this would somehow spare me some pain.

This misguided belief held true nine years later when I was living in the United States. I had found myself becoming increasingly agitated about my father's wellbeing, although I had no knowledge that he was ill. Finally, I called my mother to ask how Dad was. After a few stumbling words of reassurance, she handed the phone to my brother, who echoed her reassurances and offered me a lame explanation for why Dad could not come to the phone. He died two days later. It transpired that when I phoned, he had been calling my name as he went in and out of consciousness. I had "heard" his call.

My closest friend, Diana, and I met as seven-year-olds on a swing on Seacliff Beach, near where her family vacationed every summer. Although our homes were twenty miles apart, we were delighted to discover that we were both about to start at the same school in Adelaide. Every summer for the next seven years, Di and I enjoyed sharing our adventures on the shores and surrounding hills of Seacliff, confident in the knowledge that our friendship would continue seamlessly when we returned to school every year. At school we were inseparable, and became known as "the terrible twins." I'm not sure why we were thus identified, as I'm fairly sure that whatever mischief we got up to was pretty harmless. What I do know is that together we were a unit and united, we were fun-loving, confident, and ready to tackle new challenges. There was no secret that we could not share as we passed from childhood into early adolescence. Di developed into an attractive girl with long black hair, which she knew how to fix in countless ways. She also was skilled in the art of makeup, not to mention equally skilled in attracting the cutest boys to her side at the weekly youth dances we attended. I, on the other hand, had short, curly, dark hair which defied all attempts to style it. Although I admired Di's skills with mascara and eyeliner, I had no interest in such things myself. There was no competition, resentment, or jealousy on my part as I observed the phenomenon of boys gathered around Di like bees around a flower. It made perfect sense to me! When Diana left school in the middle of tenth grade, I was lonely and felt at a loss as to how to develop new friendships. I decided I too would leave school at the end of that year.

This upset my parents, and they immediately arranged a meeting with me and the headmistress, Mrs. Paech, to dissuade me from leaving. I was told how important it was for me to continue my education if I was to achieve what Mrs.Paech claimed was my potential for making my mark on the world. But no matter what Mrs Paech said, or my concerned parents said, I steadfastly refused to budge from my decision. Looking back, I'm impressed by my ability to resist all the pressure to which I was being subjected. So at the end of that same year, not quite fifteen years old, I dropped out of school.

Chapter 2

And so I left school at fourteen, not quite fifteen years old.

I felt lost and lonely without Diana. School had become an intolerable environment without her. Much of my unhappiness was caused by some of the popular girls who, sensing my loneliness and vulnerability, had begun to make my days miserable with frequent taunting remarks. I longed for the end of every school day, barely able to maintain my composure some days, longing for the comfort of my home and the companionship of my dogs, Trixie and Dane. Rusty had been gone about two years by this time.

Another reason for my discontent at school was that I had developed a "crush" on a boy nearly four years older than I, who was totally unaware of my existence. I couldn't wait to discard my school uniform, especially my ugly school shoes, for the freedom and independence of regular clothes, and the increased confidence I believed this would give me to have this boy notice me. I had first known David as my brother's friend when I was about eight years old, and I did not see him again until I was fourteen years old. I was one of many kids from the suburbs south of Adelaide who traveled back and forth to school on the local train. One day after school, as I sat in a window seat waiting for the train to start, David walked by. I knew him instantly, despite the intervening years—medium tall, brown curly hair, startlingly green eyes, and an athletic build. I thought he was the handsomest boy I had ever seen. After that first glimpse, I watched for him every day. I also plied my brother with questions about him, but got few answers, as they no longer hung out together. One thing I learned, though, was that he was a good friend of Jim Hardy. I also learned that Jim and David were both members of the Brighton and Seacliff Yacht Club, which was located almost directly below my home on Seacliff Beach. (Twenty years later, at the height of Jim's international competitive sailing career, Queen Elizabeth knighted Jim as one of Australia's outstanding athletes.)

My desire to know David had me considering any and all possible strategies to meet him. One of these was to frequently walk by Jim's garage, where Jim and David and several other friends were building a twelve-foot sailboat to compete in the yacht club's weekly races. The ensuing weeks of noisy electric saws, pounding hammers and frequent laughter emanating from Jim's garage were music to my ears as I invented reasons to walk by his home. Sadly, however, my efforts bore no fruit, other than sometimes exchanging a few words with Jim, and occasionally catching a glimpse of David in the background. In one of these brief exchanges with Jim, he told me that he planned to name the boat "T.M. Hardy" after his father, who had died several years before. In the early summer of 1950, the noise from across the street suddenly ceased. The boat was finished, and I had yet to meet David.

Until then, I had spent my time in competitive swimming and tennis, when I wasn't hanging out at the beach with my girlfriends...now the sport of sailing suddenly intrigued me. After telling one of the younger members of the yacht club, who I happened to know, of my growing interest in sailing, he invited me to come to the yacht club to learn what sailing was all about. This gave me the excuse I needed to visit the club frequently over the next few days. And heavenly days, only minutes after I arrived one day, I spied David rigging up a boat ready for that day's race. Despite my pounding heart, I walked over and asked him to explain to me what he was doing. Over the next few days, I found other opportunities to ask him questions and to listen with rapt attention to his every word. It probably was not hard for him to recognize how much I liked him. One day, as his green eyes smiled into my brown eyes, he took my breath away by inviting me to join the newly launched "T.M. Hardy" as his "main-sheet hand" (a nautical term for a crew member handling the mainsail). I readily agreed, barely able to contain my excitement.

And so, every weekend for four glorious summers, I competed as one of the crew of the T.M. Hardy, racing off the shores of Seacliff. Before each race, as David maneuvered our boat into position for the starting gun, I would feel the thrill of the upcoming competition and the challenges that lay ahead. David's skippering, especially in rough seas, required his total focus, and when he issued an order, he expected and got a quick response from his two-person crew—me and his friend, Bill, his forward hand. David's "ready about" meant that we needed to be ready to change course—to "gybe," going from a starboard tack to a port tack, or vice versa—in order to go with the wind. As he swung the tiller hard to the side and said "lee-o," I would duck under the mainsail as it swung over me and as Bill and I quickly switched sides. Both of us needed to loosen the lines of the mainsail and the jib as we went about, and pull them taut again as we started in the new direction. All the while David would keep his eye on the top of the mainsail. If he perceived a "wrinkle," a lack of tautness, he would respond by "luffing," moving the rudder to turn the boat to sail nearer into the wind, thus maintaining our maximum progress. The constant wet and salt-laden line running through my hands soon created calluses in the upper palm of my hands. Those calluses I thought of as my sailing "badge" and remained evident for many years after my competitive sailing days were over, a memento of those happy times.

The seas could vary from relatively mild waves and light winds to churning white crested waves with strong winds made ever more challenging for sailing small craft as intermittent strong gusts—(gully winds)—coming from the shoreline hills hit the prevailing winds. The rougher the seas and the stronger the winds, the harder I had to work—and the more I liked it! This meant "hiking" as far out on the gunwale as my body could carry me, all the while holding on to the mainsail line to keep the boat as level as possible as it rolled down into the waves. Sometimes these conditions resulted in many of the boats "pranging"—including ours—that is, capsizing into the rough seas. If we were unable to right the boat, we would wait for a rescue tow back to the distant shore.

This was all part of the joy of sailing as far as I was concerned, and I suppose, given the invincibility of youth, I felt no fear as we trod water, despite knowing that sharks could be in the area...every Aussie kid knew that the Great White shark was known to prowl the seas out from where we sailed. I was reminded of this while sailing alone one day, when I was becalmed a good distance from shore. Not wanting to spend my time sitting under the hot sun, with little hope of even a light wind to stir the sail, I straddled the bow of the boat, and began paddling toward shore. As I made slow but steady progress, I glanced into the sea just below my dangling legs in time to see a shark pass beneath them! That certainly got my attention! From then on I kept a sharp eye on the sea around me as I continued to paddle, but there were no further sightings of my marine companion.

A part of the race I particularly enjoyed was when we sailed downwind "on the run" with the wind filling the mainsail, the jib, and the spinnaker that Bill had added. This third sail enabled us to use the wind to maximum advantage. At this point, we would have a fairly clear idea of how we were doing competitively. Occasionally, we would be doing well, but most often

Sellick's Beach, 1952: Edith Whitford, Jill, David Phillips, David's sister Margaret Phillips

David and Jill, 1953

we would be in the middle or even at the end of a long line of boats. As we approached the buoy marking the race course and prepared to "go about" it, no matter where we were in relation to the other boats, I always was optimistic that the next segment of the race was an opportunity to improve our position.

In between moments of tension, I would steal secret glances at David, at his hands confidently holding the tiller, at his strong brown legs braced against the center plate, and at those green eyes constantly assessing optimum conditions for our progress.

When we weren't racing, David and I would join others in the yacht club's observation deck, watching the boats that were still racing. One day we were the only two in the lookout. As we sat side by side, not quite touching, David leaned over and brushed my lips with his! My heart began beating wildly— nothing I had known had ever felt like this. An incredibly strong sensation spread through my body. And so began our three-year romance. Thereafter, we would find opportunities to sit close, acutely aware of each other, in gatherings at the club. Sometimes we found wonderful moments alone. As I was barely fifteen, this was something I kept secret from my parents for the next year. Although in that year I was not able to go on dates with David, his buddies were all aware of our relationship, as was doubtless evident from my inability to disguise my intense feelings for him whenever I was near him.

When I turned sixteen, suddenly my parents seemed to realize that he was my sweetheart. Could it have escaped their awareness for the past year? Was it only when he came to my home to give me beautiful diamond earrings for my birthday that they noticed how important he was to me, and I to him? I think my parents had probably known all along, but had used our family "avoidance" technique to deal with the situation.

Once our relationship was officially recognized by my parents, David became a regular visitor, biking the two miles from his home in Brighton to visit me, engaging my hovering parents in polite conversation. Occasionally we would have precious moments alone. On one of these occasions, the radio was playing the song *The Night Is Young, and You're so Beautiful*. David whispered to me that that was how he thought of me, adding "when you're old you'll still be beautiful." "How do you know that?" I asked him, and he replied, "I just do."

In 1952, at age nineteen, David graduated from high school and found a job downtown. One day he surprised me by driving up in his first car, a Citroën, and from then on our social activities widened. One such new activity I especially enjoyed was driving to Sellicks Beach several miles down the coast from Seacliff for the popular car races held there. On one occasion, David's older sister, Margaret, and her boyfriend, Fred, joined us. I enjoyed their company, despite feeling shy in their presence. That was also the day that I excitedly observed the first German-made Porsche I had ever seen as it readied to compete.

David now invited me to yacht club parties, where all his friends were at least three years older than I. Most drank alcohol—many to excess—although not so David. In those days, there were few, if any, rules about drinking. It was not unusual to see someone leave a party drunk, get in their car, and weave their way home on the local roads. I never felt comfortable at these parties, being so much younger than everyone. Before going to them, I would try to think of an interesting topic I could bring up to ease my tongue-tied awkwardness, but without much success. Mostly, I hung around the periphery of conversations, all the while looking forward to the time we would be leaving. I never admitted my insecurities to David, who probably would have been helpful if I had done so.

Quite often my friend Diana would travel from her home on the north side of Adelaide and stay with me for several days at a time. Together, we would go to the yacht club, where we enjoyed hanging out with everyone. Many of David's friends were attracted to Diana, and in breaks between scheduled races, her presence invariably resulted in a great deal of fun and horseplay. Diana, whose last name was Benson, acquired the nickname "Basher Benson" as a result of her habit of punching a boy she especially liked a bit too hard in her enthusiasm to interact with him. When not much was happening at the club, I can still picture Diana and me, in our tiny white shorts, walk-

Jill and David, 1952

ing from the yacht club to Brighton Beach a mile or so down the coast, as we shared our thoughts and secrets, happy to be together.

Occasionally David would invite Diana to accompany us to a social activity in the city. On these occasions, he had a surprising amount of patience with us, as often Diana and I regressed into two giggly teenagers. Sometimes, he would drive with the two of us sitting in the back seat, laughing at some obscure joke, and I would catch his green eyes looking at us in his rear view mirror. In those moments I would be aware of our large age difference, and he would feel more like an older brother than my sweetheart.

My only personal experience with drinking alcohol was on a hot summer day when David and I were with friends sitting under umbrellas in the Seacliff Hotel beer garden. Perhaps as a way to fit in I ordered a gin and tonic, which I drank quickly to quench my thirst. I soon began to feel strangely unwell and told David I was going home, by myself. I arrived there five minutes later. My mother met me at the front door, and after I had spoken no more than two or three words, her horrified reaction was to say, "Jill, you're drunk!" Right then and there she extracted a promise from me that I would not drink alcohol; I can't remember for how long. I kept my promise until I started my nursing training two years later, at which time I gave it no further thought.

More enjoyable for me than the parties were the occasional times when many of the yacht club crowd, as a group, attended charity balls in the city. The boys would wear their best clothes, and the girls would wear long dresses. (I had taught myself to sew on my mother's Singer sewing machine, and had become skilled at making my own clothes, including dresses for such occasions.) I would feel at ease as David and I danced the night away to big band music. Whenever I hear tunes such as *Up the Lazy River by the Old Mill Stream*, or *I'll See You In My Dreams*, or *All of Me*, I am right back there cruising around the dance floor with David, my green-eyed sweetheart.

In those days it was considered a rite of passage to be a debutante and to be formally presented into society. In my floor-length dress of tulle and lace, which I had sewn for the occasion, and holding David's arm, I followed several other couples across the dance floor, as each of us in turn was "presented" to the mayor of Adelaide at the annual Red Cross Charity Ball. It all seems terribly quaint to think of that night now, but at sixteen years old, I was following the expectations of the world in which I lived. I was fortunate to know David at that time in my life. He was always thoughtful and kind to me, and helped guide me through those years in ways that significantly increased my self-confidence as I grew into young womanhood.

At the age of eighteen, bored with my job as a shorthand typist, I decided to go into nursing training. Once I began my training, David and I gradually saw less and less of each other, and eventually we went our separate ways. Our paths rarely crossed over the years, although we shared a few mutual friends scattered over Australia, and I heard news of him from time to time. The last time I saw him was in 1959, by an amazing coincidence, at the top of Mt. Kosciuszko ski slopes in the Australian Alps. This was shortly before I left to work as a nurse in the United States. Off to the side from the others, we talked for only a few minutes, and then we said goodbye. He was still medium tall, dark, and handsome, and his eyes were as green and beautiful as ever.

On April 12, 1954, one month after my eighteenth birthday, I gathered with fourteen other young women in a meeting room in the nurses' residence of the Adelaide Children's Hospital. We henceforth were to be known as members of the 45th Preliminary Training School (45th PTS), and we always proudly identified ourselves as "we of the 45th." We were awaiting the arrival of our tutor, Sister Carroll (in the British system, all registered nurses are addressed as Sister) who was to orient us as to what to expect as probationary student nurses.

Just minutes before, I had been shown to what was to be my room for the next three months. If I successfully passed my probationary period, it would continue to be my assigned room on the first floor of the nurses' residence. I was excited, imagining what lay ahead, and was delighted with my little room, which consisted of a single bed, a small table, and a chest of drawers with a mirror—the first time in my life I was to have the privacy of my own bedroom.

In response to the sound of many voices going by, I opened my door to the outside hallway, and as I did so, the door of the room on my right had also opened. A tall girl with blond hair and beautiful blue eyes accented by amazingly long, black eyelashes, stood there. "Hello, I'm Beth," she said, and "Hello, I'm Jill," I replied. So began what was to be our lifelong friendship.

Jill and Beth Harvey, RNs, April 12, 1957, Graduate Nurses

And so also began one of the best three years of my life. As probationary nurses we spent several hours a day in class and the remainder on the wards doing unpleasant tasks, such as scrubbing bedpans or cleaning beds and cots with disinfectants. Having never worked so hard in my life, this was a severe shock to my system. It also turned my hands into rough, sometimes bleeding, appendages.

I would go home on my one day off a week, smother olive oil on them, and encase them in cotton gloves before going to bed at night. My mother cooking my favorite foods and my being back by the sea more than compensated for the discomfort of my hands and helped rejuvenate me for the coming week.

One day on the wards, I observed a procedure on a child involving cleaning a nasty infected leg wound. I felt dizzy and slid to the floor in a faint. The next day Sister Carroll gently informed me, "Nurse Griffiths, if you are serious about becoming a trained nurse, you cannot faint!" I took her words to heart, and learned to ignore my lurching stomach in the many challenging situations that I encountered from that day on.

In truth, there was one more occasion when I fainted, but by that time I was a senior student, and in no danger of being dismissed from the program. I was the operating room nurse assisting an ophthalmic surgeon removing a child's severely injured eye. As his knife dug beneath the eye and blood oozed around the site, I felt light-headed and broke into a sweat. Fortunately, I had the presence of mind to hand my suction instrument to the assistant next to me and to fall backwards, away from the operating table. My next awareness was of lying on a stretcher, with said surgeon anxiously bending over me and asking "Are you okay?" Of course I was fine, but terribly embarrassed—not my finest hour as a nurse! Although there were many other times throughout my nursing career when I felt affected by horrific situations, I never again fainted.

Once past our probationary period, we were each assigned to wards throughout the hospital, which treated the sickest children from around the state. We usually began work at 5.30 a.m., six days a week, breaking for breakfast at 7 a.m. before returning to the wards. This was a time to catch up with other members of the "45th," compare our experiences, discuss graphic details of such things as pungent bodily fluids and pustulant wounds, even as we gulped our food. Often we were on what was known as split shifts, so that we might work until 10 p.m. that night to fulfill the quota of our eight-hour day.

Every three months or so, we were scheduled to work a month on the night shift, a quiet world of shaded lights and muffled sounds, where very sick children seemed a little less able to cling to life.

Critically ill or dying children facing their own mortality frequently humbled me with their courage and spiritual calm, but of the many, one child stands out in my memory. Diane was about eight years old when she was admitted to the burn ward a few months after I started my training. She had been at a party wearing a special lace dress for the occasion when another child had thrown a firecracker at her, which had immediately ignited her clothing. By the time the adults present put out the flames, 80% of her body had been badly burned. Every time I was assigned to the burn ward, I knew Diane would be there, enduring significant pain, which was barely diminished by injections of morphine, as she underwent daily treatment and periodic skin grafts. Even as I braced myself to change the dressings on her tortured body, I was filled with admiration for this little girl's bravery, who barely whimpered throughout the painful process. With only two or three weeks left before I graduated as a registered nurse, I learned that Diane, after nearly three years of hospitalization, was finally healed and ready for discharge into the outside world. I joined many members of the nursing and medical staff who gathered to hug Diane goodbye as she prepared to walk out of the hospital with her parents. Her long-sleeved dress covered most of her disfiguring scars, and her face, which mercifully escaped the flames, shone with happiness. I hoped that her life would be the rewarding one she so deserved.

As we were rotated through the different wards, and as our nursing skills and knowledge became more solid, we were given increased responsibilities.

By our third year of training, we were put second in charge of a ward, the first in charge being a registered nurse. Between shifts, or on our one day off a week, we were required to attend and periodically to be tested on all required lectures. Despite the hard work, long hours, and emotionally and physically challenging situations, I loved my life as a student nurse.

From that very first day, and despite our differences, Beth and I were friends, she the farm girl skilled in everything from driving tractors to auto mechanics, and me, the city girl, having no such skills. Nevertheless, we found much in common, including our love of nature and animals and an appreciation for the simple things of life. Whenever possible we visited the farm, where we helped with the many chores, joined the dogs in rounding up the sheep, rode horses, and ate enormous amounts of her mother's cooking. At night, sleeping in her absent brother's bed, my dreams were colored with fantasies of romance with him. I never told Beth about my crush on her handsome brother. Despite my flourishing love life over those years, John never showed any interest in me, and I never acknowledged my attraction to him.

Life in the nurses' residence was a greatly different life from the one I had previously known. Although we were all over eighteen, we lived there under strict rules of discipline, with a midnight curfew. No men were allowed past the reception area on the ground floor. Many of us viewed this as a personal challenge and managed to sneak the occasional boyfriend past the watchful eyes of the live-in watchdog, Sister "Bloody Mary" Connors.

Many strategies were developed to bypass these curfew rules, including blocking a door open in anticipation of someone's return past midnight or agreeing to leave a bedroom window open for someone to climb through as needed. One memorable night, one of those strategies went badly wrong!

In the early morning hours my sleep was shattered by the sound of breaking glass, as my friend, Melanie, came crashing through my window, barely missing me as she landed on my bed, hit the floor running, and disappeared into the hallway beyond. As I turned on my light, carefully avoiding the broken glass around me, I realized two things: one was that I had forgotten to leave my window open as I had promised Melanie I would, and the other was a trail of blood that led from my bed and across the floor to the open door. In the next few moments I became aware of a great deal of shouting and screaming farther down the hall, followed by an eerie silence. Bloody Mary, hot on Melanie's trail, had followed the blood down the hallway and apprehended her! The punishment meted out for Melanie's bad behavior was to write 2,000 times: "I must always obey the rules of the Residence for my own safety." Melanie, none the worse for her misadventure, insisted it was only fair that I should fulfill this assignment, given my lack of responsibility in not opening my window as promised. I agreed to do this, if only to assuage my own guilt, and I did so in record time by taping five or six pens together as I covered each page with the assigned sentence. The irony of these situations was not lost on us: on the one hand we were treated as naughty schoolgirls; on the other, we were assigned the huge responsibility of caring for very sick children every day as we progressed through our training.

There was a telephone on each of the residence's six floors. They rang constantly, followed by someone yelling down the hallway for the person being called. Some of the best times I experienced in my first year of training was when the "woolies" came to town. These were the buyers of high quality Merino wool, one of Australia's primary industries at the time. The woolies were all young men, eager for a good time, on what seemed to be unlimited expense accounts. Whenever they called, my friends and I were more than ready to join them. My promise to my mother to not drink was forgotten as I showed off my ability to win in many a drinking game. Fortunately, I did not experience any bad consequences because of my behavior. One of the woolies, John, a few years older than I, much to my surprise, one night asked me to marry him. I managed to preserve my composure and his ego as I politely turned him down.

Another ready source of male admirers were the young doctors that we worked side by side with every day. As my nursing skills developed, so did my self-confidence in my interactions with them and my ability to flirt with the ones I found to my liking. After a night of socializing I would often find myself the next day interacting with my date of the night before in a staff meeting or at the bedside of a sick child. As we exchanged medical informa-tion, our manner with each other would give no hint of the previous night's activities as we maintained our professional demeanor. I always enjoyed these situations enormously, as I suspect the other person did, too. All of us were young and all of us worked hard every day. But we were also ready to enjoy life vigorously in our off-duty time, and not a few romances blossomed into marriage. Although I liked and enjoyed the excitement of dating these young doctors, I had no desire to make any permanent commitment. I had my long-range plans, which were to stay single and to explore the wide world beyond my familiar shores.

Beth and I completed our training on the same day, April 12, 1957. We were ready to take the next step, one year's postgraduate training. We decided to do this training in Perth, the capital of Western Australia, which we had visited by ship across the Southern Ocean the previous year. We had fallen in love with this beautiful city on the Swan River, where literally hundreds of black swans wandered its banks, and which was close to miles of sandy beaches. Other than a vacation we had taken together after our first year of training to Mt. Buffalo in the state of Victoria, this was the only place either of us had ever visited outside our home state. So Perth it was!

Our first six months of training were in adult nursing at the Royal Perth General Hospital, where for the first time Beth and I shared a room. One way Beth was unlike me was that at 5:30 in the morning, she was a grouch, whereas I awoke as the pleasantest of persons, full of cheerful chatter. After ignoring several of Beth's warnings to stop talking to her so early in the morning, I realized the sincerity of her words the second or third morning in our new home. As she pulled on her black stockings, she shouted, "Don't say another bloody word until after we have had breakfast!" After a shocked second or two of silence on my part, I managed to reply, "Okay, okay, I get it!" In that instant I learned that recounting details of the previous night's dreams held no fascination for her.

Taking care of adult patients was an entirely different experience from pediatric nursing. Many of the men were World War II veterans, and some of them had serious medical conditions. Nevertheless, they enjoyed flirting with the young nurses attending to their needs, and I was always appreciative of their sense of humor, often laughing at their jokes as I took care of them. Some were good raconteurs of their lives during the war years. Although they never talked of any serious experiences, I sometimes sensed underlying emotions that they skirted. I knew it was typical behavior of that generation in a world that expected men to demonstrate their strength by never acknowledging their inner struggles and fears. One man told me about "jungle juice," an alcoholic concoction made out of anything available, such as kerosene, that many of them drank, despite knowing it could result in serious physical problems, such as blindness and liver damage. Indeed, I became abruptly and frighteningly aware of alcohol dependency issues one night when a patient went into what was known as delirium tremens (DTs), screaming in terror at the creatures he perceived crawling on the walls around him. In those days, there was little knowledge about alcoholism treatment, other than in such situations to heavily sedate the person.

As fourth-year nurses, we had four stripes on our sleeves, and the men loved to kid us by calling us "sergeant major" to get our attention. One creative man presented me with a drawing that portrayed me as a kangaroo in my nursing uniform, including my veil, white apron, and the four stripes on my sleeve, bouncing over the floor. Sixty years later, I still have that drawing.

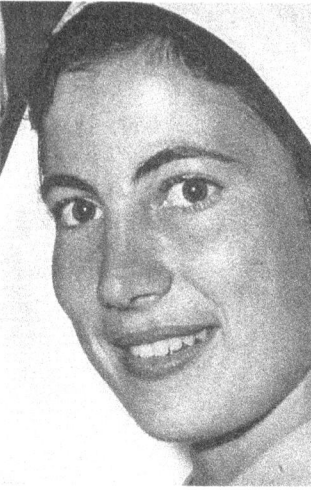

Jillian, RN, 1958

*Cartoon drawn by a patient at Royal
Perth Hospital, 1957*

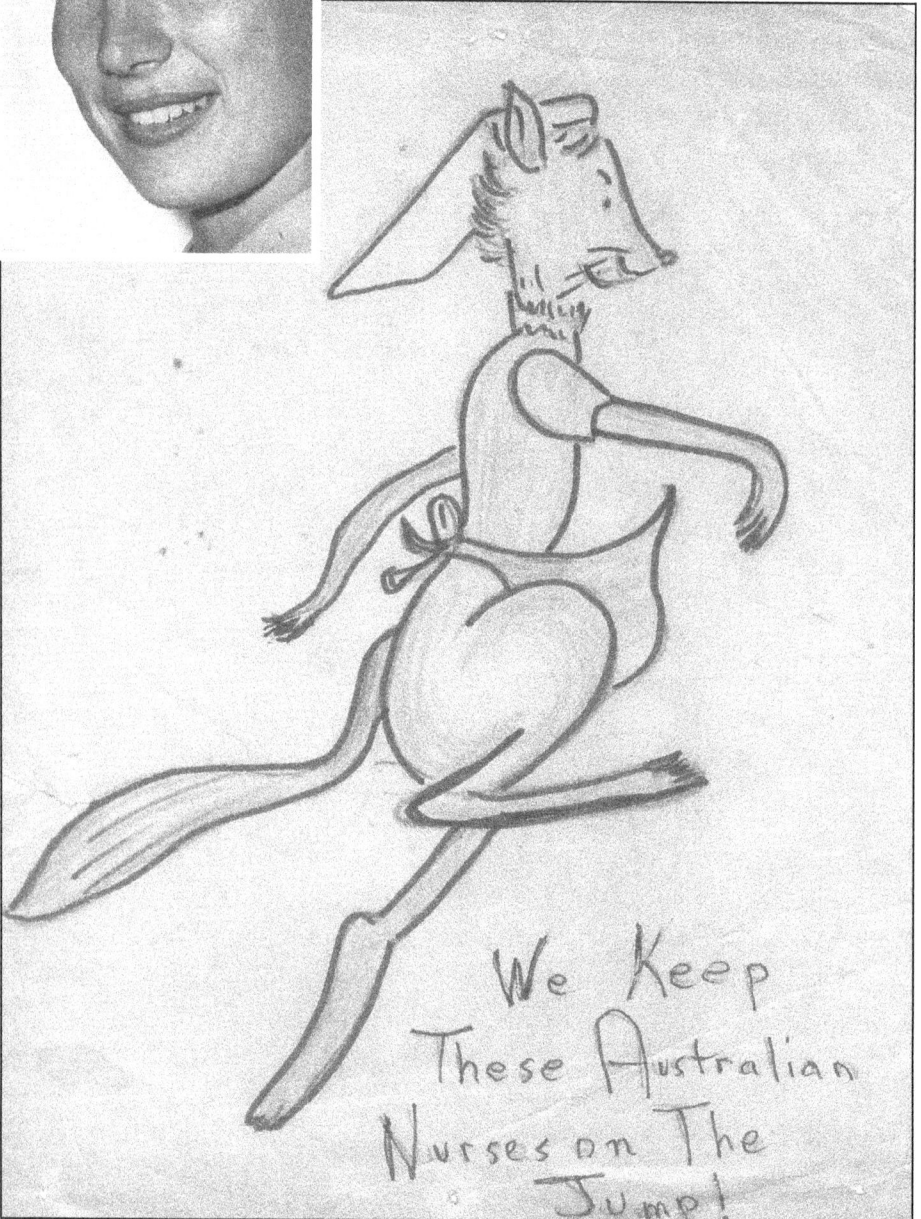

We Keep
These Australian
Nurses on The
Jump!

I found taking care of female patients was very different from caring for male patients. The older women tended to be modest and uncomplaining and to keep much to themselves. However, when I found the time to sit by a bedside and encourage a woman to talk about herself, I was surprised to find that many of them had lived very interesting lives. As a twenty-one-year-old, I had assumed otherwise. This was a new awareness: to realize that they had once been young and vital. One woman in particular told me how much she had loved playing sports, something that had not occurred to me as I observed her frail and aging body. A much younger woman told me that she had had several children, and because of her religion she had learned to dread sex with her husband for fear of having another child. This was a shocking thought for me; I couldn't imagine dreading sex. Another young woman was recovering from having aborted her pregnancy, a criminal offense in those days. On her discharge from the hospital, she knew she was facing legal charges and almost certain jail time for her actions. This was at a time before "the pill," and women had no sure way to protect themselves against pregnancy. This woman's troubles caused me to feel great sympathy for her and to have plenty to think about personally.

For our second six months of training, Beth and I began work as staff nurses at the Princess Margaret Children's Hospital, which served the sickest children in Western Australia.

By then it was December, the height of the Australian summer, with temperatures frequently over 100°F. Many of the children who came in were severely dehydrated as a result of acute diarrhea. Other children came in with extremely high temperatures—I recall a child coming in with a temperature of 108°F. Even after being packed in ice, this child did not survive. On occasion, a critically ill child would be admitted with severe tetanus disease. This was before the advent of a tetanus vaccine, and the only treatment available was an intravenous cocktail of sedatives and antibiotics, a quiet location, and skilled nursing care. We had signs posted outside the hospital urging motorists not to use their car horns, as sudden noise could precipitate severe muscle spasms and rigidity. These spasms could involve the neck and throat, as well as the back muscles, and were not only extremely painful, but could result in broken bones, joint dislocation, respiratory failure due to a lack of oxygen, and, often, death. A severe spasm involving the neck and the back could result in what is known as opisthotonus—a truly awful condition with the back arched—the only parts of the child's body touching the bed were the back of the head, and the heels of the feet. At least half of these children died

Row 3: Jill, second to end, right; Beth, end, right, 1957

despite our best efforts. Although these six months were postgraduate training for me, I was titled a staff nurse and given considerably more responsibility than I had experienced in my student nursing training. I learned a great deal, and at the completion of my time at Princess Margaret Hospital, I felt ready for the responsibility of a charge nurse of a ward.

Our time off in those hot summer days was spent as much as possible on local golden-sanded beaches, one of our favorite places being the nearby and popular Cottesloe Beach. Beth and I, as staff nurses, were no longer eligible for nurses' residential living, so we found a comfortable house to rent in a suburb named Hollywood. Our home soon became a gathering spot for many of the people we had met since arriving in Perth.

Another favorite place to spend time was King's Park, one of the largest inner-city parks in the world, and home to more than half of Australia's 25,000 plant species. Western Australia is known for an abundance of wildflowers, with thousands of plant species that live nowhere else in the world. Flowering trees and flowers of all colors grow in the park, and as many of the plants are pollinated by birds, an added delight was to see many birds flying from one plant to another. Occasionally, we found time to attend one of the live outdoor music concerts, the enjoyment greatly enhanced by its glorious setting.

When taking advantage of King's Park's great hiking trails or other hiking trails, we Aussies gave little thought to the many things that can kill you in extremely nasty ways, perhaps unlike visitors to the land known to the rest of the world as Down Under. These creatures included highly venomous spiders such as the Sydney Funnel Web (allegedly the world's deadliest, which one time had dropped down to the ground at my feet as I opened a screen door), and the Redback spider, (which I'd seen and examined with caution as a child when playing outdoors). Of the world's most venomous snakes, Australia has the top three most venomous. One of these, the Eastern Brown, my mother once found my five-year-old self offering "a nice drink of milk" outside our back gate. The other two most venomous snakes are the Inland Taipan and the Tiger. Most snakes don't want to hurt you, but Aussie folk wisdom is that if you're hiking in the bush and a snake comes along, just stay still and quiet and you'll probably survive the encounter.

Yet another favorite place to play was on Rottnest Island, off the coast of Fremantle, south of Perth and reachable by a 45-minute ferry ride. Rottnest, with a permanent population of about 300 people, is a sandy, low-lying island, which had separated from the mainland around 7,000 years before, and where human artifacts had been found dating back at least 30,000 years. The island was well known for its population of quokkas, a small native marsupial found in few other locations. Although we did not see any quokkas while we were there, we did observe sea lions and fur seals that also made their homes there. Only bikes were allowed for transportation—no cars—so life was simple away from the city lights. Many of the island's huts, some of which we stayed in, dated from the British colonial period in the early 1800s, when the island was used as a military installation. While there, we played beach games, surfed, walked the trails, and partied with friends.

All too soon, our year in Western Australia was up, and it was time to decide "what next?" We returned to Adelaide by train across the desert of the Nullarbor Plains, enjoying a surprising closeness with many of the other passengers over those three days of isolation from the rest of the world. After a few weeks back in Adelaide, we decided "what next" was Sydney. Two or three days later we flew into Sydney, with no plans, but with every confidence that this would be yet another enjoyable adventure.

In our first week there, we found employment at a local hospital, sharing an efficiency apartment with another nursing friend, Carmel Gilbert (Gillie). As there were only two twin beds, we developed a system, which worked reasonably well as we all worked different shifts: whoever wasn't working gained possession of the available bed. Happily though, we soon found a really attractive house to rent in Mosman, a Sydney suburb, on a cliff over-looking Sydney Harbor and the famous Sydney Harbor Bridge. To get to and from our work in Sydney we would catch the ferry below, easily accessed on a winding path down the cliffside. The ferry ride to work at sunrise and the return trip at dusk, with the beauty of the sunrises and sunsets reflected on the water, were the best part of every day.

Sydney more than lived up to our expectations. Visiting Kings Cross was exciting and a little shocking, where the "red light" business of organized crime coexisted with drag queens, bohemian living, and alternate lifestyles formerly unknown to us. The Art Gallery of New South Wales was my intro-duction to world-famous art. The Taronga Park Zoo, with its incredible harbor view and widely diverse array of animals from all over the world, made our Adelaide Zoo seem quaint in comparison. Surfing at the world-famous Bondi Beach and sailing on Sydney Harbor and through Bradley Heads to the Pacific Ocean, or past The Gap, renowned as the scene of countless suicides, were memorable experiences.

One of the best memories I have is of my mother joining me for a trip to the Blue Mountains National Park, west of Sydney, part of the Great Dividing Range. We drove through tree-covered mountains, home of lyrebirds and crimson rosella parrots, to Echo Point lookout with a panoramic view of the Three Sisters, a towering sandstone formation and sacred Aboriginal site. This was my mother's first time traveling out of South Australia, and it was a lovely time that we were able to share.

Another memory comes to mind. On a certain summer day a French ship docked in Sydney Harbor, and it was quite the sight to see the French sailors with their red pompons on their sailor hats bobbing all over the Sydney streets. I was walking with my English friend, Patricia Lewis, who worked as a secretary in a Sydney-based insurance company. I had known Patricia since my pre-nursing days in Adelaide when I had worked as a shorthand typist and she was my supervisor, and she had recently become our fourth house-mate in our home. We were both enjoying the sight of hundreds of sailors swarming through the streets when I had an idea: let's get to know a couple! Patricia, much more conservatively behaved than I, at first resisted the idea, but with some persuasion, she agreed to give it a go. Catching the eyes of two good-looking young sailors, we struck up a conversation using our schoolgirl French, and they in turn responded to us with their limited English. We were having such a good time that we invited them to accompany us to our home, to which they readily agreed. After crossing the harbor by ferry and walking up the cliff to our home, they seemed happy to meet Beth and Gillie. I don't remember what we cooked for dinner that night, but I do remember sipping red wine and sharing lots of laughter with them all evening. Then it was time for them to make their way back to their ship. As we watched them walking

My brother's family circa 1960: Bronwyn, Susie, Peg with baby Deb, David, Paul

down the cliff path, they turned just once and waved to us before reaching the ferry. It had been an enjoyable experience for us all.

Shortly after renting our house we decided to throw a housewarming party and invited the few people we already knew, asking them to bring a friend or two to swell the numbers. Two of the early arrivals were two tall, handsome, athletic-looking guys, Barry Rush and Tim Cox. Beth and I exchanged looks with each other, wordlessly agreeing that we would like to get to know these two. By the end of the evening we had matched up, Beth and Tim, and Barry and I. Beth and Tim had a short-lived friendship, but for the remainder of my year in Sydney, Barry and I enjoyed a fun romance as well as a close friendship. Barry was a commercial pilot, and although we maintained our relationship for a while after I left Sydney, after he began flying for a Malaysian airline, we eventually lost contact.

After a year in Sydney, in mid-1959, Beth and I returned to Adelaide, both of us having accepted positions as charge nurses at Adelaide Children's Hospital (ACH), she in the operating room, and I in the emergency department and surgical clinics. This was a whole new experience for both of us as charge nurses, with all the responsibility that entailed. For the next two years we enjoyed the life of working hard, and, in our time off, playing hard. With two other nursing friends, Pam Dighton and Rosie Porter, we rented a house on Hackney Road on the outskirts of the city, within walking distance of the hospital. This house soon became a center of social activity, as people came and went, whether all four of us were there or not. Nevertheless, despite the seemingly endless partying, things never got out of hand, and the availability of alcohol was limited, as we four friends were much more interested in music and dancing than we were in drinking.

Over these two years, I strengthened my friendship with Harry Burnell, a young doctor I had met at the ACH before going to Sydney, and who had occasionally visited me there. Life started to feel complicated for me as my feelings for Harry deepened. There were many adventures waiting for me out there in the world, and I knew with certainty that I wanted to find them. Even as many of my friends began to marry and settle down, I knew that was not for me at this time in my life.

One day, in conversation with Pam, we talked of how much we had always wanted to travel. One thing led to another, and we impulsively decided to put our thoughts into action. In a seemingly short time, after making our applications for postgraduate nursing assignments in the U.S.—a country I had always wanted to visit, unlike most of my friends who invariably preferred visiting the U.K.—we received notification that we had been accepted into a

The s.s. Orcades. As a two class ship, she provided accommodation for 773 First Class and 772 tourist class passengers.

two-year contract sponsored by the American Nurses Association. Our first assignment was to be at Johns Hopkins Hospital in Baltimore, Maryland, and our second assignment was to be at the University of Colorado in Denver. Our contract started April 12, 1961, exactly seven years after I had started my nursing training in 1954, and exactly four years after I had finished that training. This seemed like a good omen to me.

In retrospect, I realize how insensitive I was as to how my plans might affect others, Harry in particular. In typical Australian male style, he did not verbalize to me his sense of loss at my leaving for two years. As it transpired, I did not return to Australia for five years. In 1965 he married a nurse he met at the ACH.

After much preparation Pam and I were ready to set out on this exciting adventure, having no idea where it would lead us. In late February 1961, shortly before my 25th birthday, we said farewell to our families and friends at the Adelaide airport. I would not see Beth again until October 1964, in Denver, just before the birth of Matthew, my first child. My parents and my brother David and his wife Peg and my sister Mary were there, and all seemed happy for me as they said their farewells, believing as I did that I would be returning in two years. We flew to Sydney more than ready to join the s.s. Orcades on its three-week sail across the Pacific to the United States.

While in Sydney for few days, we caught up with our Sydney friends and visited some of our old haunts. It was lovely to see everyone again, and our pleasure was heightened by the anticipation of our upcoming American adventure. Most of my impressions of America I had gleaned from my fascination with American movies—most of these impressions unrealistic—that America was a country of wealthy people living relatively easy, carefree lives, as well as a country with crime-ridden streets. As our friends stood on the Sydney wharf to wave goodbye, I was thrilled to imagine what lay ahead—not only exploring the exciting, romantic land of America, but my anticipation of working in one of the world's great hospitals, with doctors and nurses from all over the world.

Chapter 3

As a child I had a recurring dream: I was flying high above land on a magic carpet. When I looked down, I saw many varied scenes: jungles, rivers, people, and animals below that captured my attention. In every dream, as my eyes were drawn to the scenes below, my carpet would gradually lose altitude, until I was desperately trying not to hit the ground. I would awaken just before I was about to crash. Australia to me had always felt remote from the rest of the world. As the ship pulled away from the Sydney wharf, I felt my dream was coming true. I was about to see and experience many new people and places.

Although Pam and I were traveling tourist class, as we thoroughly explored this huge ship we experienced what felt like a promise of three weeks of luxury. The several levels of the *s.s. Orcades* decks crackled with smartly dressed waiters serving food and drinks to the passengers. Dining, snack, and drink areas intermixed with groups playing deck games, lounging in chairs, or just hanging over the rails staring out to sea. Tennis courts, table tennis, a swimming pool, a library, and a movie theater beckoned us. Over the ensuing days, Pam and I entered many contests, including the table tennis tournament. Pam was champion of the tournament, and I the runner-up. At one of the many evening activities, Pam's "fancy dress" costume won first prize for originality. My costume, called "Miss Tie Land," consisting of about a dozen ties borrowed from male passengers, received only a smattering of polite applause.

Almost every day I played chess with a man in his mid-thirties. Although I enjoyed playing him, I never won, just as it had been the countless times with my father. He reminded me of Dad in other ways, too; older men had always attracted me. Why did he keep inviting me back, and what kept drawing me back? Was it his quiet good looks? He was far more sophisticated than I, yet he enjoyed my company, in retrospect, much as Dad had been attracted to

Jillian's "Tie dress"

Mother, 22 years younger than he. At the end of the trip, he admitted that he was a champion chess player from a town in New South Wales. We went our separate ways, and although I cannot recall his name, I remember him.

Our first port of call was Fiji, which was our introduction to an entirely new culture. The weather was perfect; warm and sunny, with a gentle sea breeze. The people we met were soft spoken and friendly, and my most vivid memory as we sat under the swaying tropical trees was to watch them roast a large pig in an earth oven. The outcome of this was the most delicious meal I had ever eaten.

We enjoyed several more fun-filled days crossing the Pacific Ocean, including the drama of crossing the International Date Line, where we gained a whole day in our lives. Our ship next berthed in Oahu, one of the Hawaiian islands. While there for two days, we visited Diamond Head Beach and "boogie boarded" in the world-famous surf. At one point, wanting to buy a soft drink, I asked for "a Coke." Because of my strong Australian accent, no one could understand what I was asking for. After several unsuccessful attempts to be understood, in exasperation I demanded "a Coca Cola," and with relief received my drink.

On the last few days of our Pacific crossing, one of our new friends brought out his ham radio and was able to pick up a radio show on the West Coast of America. We all gathered around him in excited reaction to hearing American accents and the realization of how close we were to our destination. Three days later we crossed under the Golden Gate Bridge. What a sight! San Francisco, a city we had heard so much about. It became, and has remained, one of my favorite cities in the world (the other two are Perth and New Orleans). Then the ship turned north to Vancouver, Canada. We spent two days exploring the city, which seemed to be full of Australians, before rejoining the ship, which headed back down the Pacific coast. After again stopping briefly in San Francisco, the *s.s. Orcades* continued to Los Angeles, where we disembarked. It was four days after my 25th birthday. We had three weeks to explore America.

Pam and I agreed that we wanted to travel by Greyhound bus. Unlike air travel, this would allow us to better know the people and the land of this fabulous country. Our first destination was Las Vegas. Accordingly, we boarded a bus out of Los Angeles. We quickly got into a conversation with a man in his early thirties. He turned out to be headed for the gaming tables of Las Vegas as a "shill." He described his job was to lure people into gambling away as much of their money as possible. He assured us that the "house" always won in the end! Once we reached Las Vegas, perhaps influenced by his rhetoric, I took an instant dislike to the atmosphere of high-stakes gambling. I was convinced that everyone I saw was suffering the desolation of having lost all their possessions. Despite shows headlined by celebrity entertainers, I couldn't wait to leave. This was a heartless town. I have never returned.

In New Mexico, the towering mountains and the desert flowers enchanted us. We especially loved the simple beauty of the colored adobe houses. Santa Fe cast a strong sense of spirituality over us as we trod the ancient stones of the historical old churches. In Taos I bought four woven tablemats from the man I had been watching weave them on his loom. He told me that their eagle emblem was the same design as the mats he was commissioned to make for President John F. Kennedy! Intrigued by the romance of our surroundings, we both bought original paintings by local artists. My painting, *Quatre Vents* by Erik Gibberd, which I bought for $300, has increased in value to well over $2,000. At the time, we had very little cash. We both bought our paintings on a monthly payment plan; mine took me three years to pay off.

In our travels, after crisscrossing many states, briefly going back into Canada to visit Niagara Falls and Toronto, we once again turned south. We travelled down the East Coast, visiting historical sites in Philadelphia, the city of brotherly love. We left Philadelphia for New York City with only five days remaining before starting our new jobs on April 12. Over the course of the previous weeks, we had met and talked with people from many walks of life. Most of them were interested in getting to know us. Almost without fail, they commented on three things: how much they enjoyed our accents; whether we had kangaroos hopping down the street where we lived in Australia; how much they had always wanted to go to Australia. If I could have had a nickel for every time someone had told me the latter, I would have become rich over the nearly sixty years I have lived in America. One man also commented on how much he liked my teeth, actually asking me if they were "store bought." He qualified this remark by telling me he had been on "R & R" (rest and relaxation) in Australia during his service in the U.S. Army in World War II, and had been struck by the bad teeth of most Australians.

On April 11, 1961, we moved our sparse belongings into Hampton House, the nurses' residence across from the Johns Hopkins Hospital (JHH) on Broadway. On April 12 we reported for duty, and once again, this significant date occurred in my life.

I had several strong impressions during my orientation to JHH. One was seeing the huge statue of Jesus in the hospital's entry. This statue surprised me, and I wondered at its implications in a nonreligious hospital. Perhaps it was my first real awareness of the depth of religious beliefs among the majority of Americans. Fifty years later I visited Johns Hopkins with my friend Marilyn Mandler, a JHH alumna, for a reunion. At this reunion I was delighted to become reacquainted with Allie, who had been my head nurse while I was at JHH in 1961, and who I had not seen since. As the three of us stood by the statue of Jesus and had a passerby take our picture, I once again pondered what message it may convey to each person who viewed it. To me it conveyed a message of love in the face of suffering and comfort in a time of loss.

Another strong impression during my orientation at JHH was the extreme, even excessive, sense of pride conveyed by the staff as they extolled the history and virtues of the university and hospital. This was not lost on Pam and me, and we both felt somewhat affronted by what felt like an inflated sense of pride. Perhaps our reaction was partly due to the difference between our more laid-back Australian culture and the dynamic American attitude of high energy and sense of superiority.

As a healthy eater, I was surprised to see medical personnel eating junk food, such as donuts and Coca Cola for breakfast, and milk with their other meals; I had never seen grown men drink milk before.

As I began to feel more comfortable sharing meals with the medical staff, another memory stands out for me. Dr. Charles Hatcher, a surgeon from Georgia, with a strong accent and a wonderful sense of humor, loved to tell jokes. Not infrequently, after he had delivered his punch line, someone would turn to me with a "what did he say?" before they felt able to laugh. This struck me as ironic. As a person from another country, I could understand this man's words better than his fellow citizens. Was it because of all the American movies I had watched in the past, or was I just more skilled in understanding accents other than my own?

My first days on the surgical intensive unit were definitely a personal challenge as I adjusted to the intense schedule. These postsurgical patients needed to be closely monitored and stabilized before being transferred to other areas of the hospital. While working there, I had continued to wear the veil of an Australian RN, and I remember more than one patient's reaction as they regained consciousness. "Tell me you are not a nun," and another: "Have I died and gone to Heaven?"

One of my first patients was an inebriated man who had been admitted with abdominal stab wounds. As I took his vital signs every 15 minutes, I was nearly overpowered by the alcoholic odor emanating from the pores of his skin, as well as unnerved on observing pubic lice as I examined his abdominal dressing! Happily he lived, and I gained my first acquaintance with the extreme poverty and related high levels of violence of inner-city living in the United States.

Once while I was monitoring a patient I became aware of someone standing motionless behind me. On completing my medical checks, I turned around to see Dr. James Jude, the person recognized as having developed the then-new method of cardiopulmonary resuscitation (CPR), watching me! Our eyes met, but without comment he turned and walked away. Presumably he was satisfied with what he had observed. Much to my relief I apparently passed the test of the ultimate tester!

Working at JHH was to occasionally find myself in the presence of world-renowned physicians, sometimes on the surgical unit where I was working or by attending a lecture. Most memorably, however, were the times I watched the operating room below from the observation tower above. This allowed me to actually see a surgeon whom I had read about in my textbooks doing the actual procedure for which he was acclaimed!

I made many new friends while at JHH, most of whom lived in row houses, and whom I would walk a mile or two to visit. One hot evening I must have taken a wrong turn, and it soon became clear that I was in unfamiliar surroundings. As I passed street after street of row houses I became aware that the people sitting on their front stoops were all African Americans. As they had watched me go by, no one indicated a particular interest in me, and no one made any attempt to talk with me. On my part, I felt irritated at being lost and late to meet my friends, but I felt no reason to be afraid. Suddenly a police car pulled up beside me. The lone white policeman rolled down his window and asked me what I thought I was doing. I replied that I was lost, and his curt response was, "Get in!" I obediently complied. While driving me back to the street I had been seeking, he informed me that I had been putting myself in danger. He qualified this by telling me that where he had found me was an unsafe neighborhood, and warned me to be more careful in the future.

A Canadian doctor I was dating, Paul Goode, like all the doctors in training at JHH, worked long hours, and it was sometimes difficult for us to find time together. One day, when I mentioned I would like to go to Washington, D.C., Paul surprised me by suggesting that I could borrow his car to drive myself there. This car was his pride and joy, a snazzy red sports beauty. Coming from Australia, one of the few countries in the world where cars were driven on the left, I had never driven on the "wrong" side of the road. I chose to not mention this minor detail and happily accepted his offer. Given his schedule and my enthusiasm for driving his car, I managed to twice drive myself to Washington in the next few weeks, the first time to enjoy the incredible beauty of Washington's cherry blossoms and the second time to visit the White House and the Lincoln Memorial. Admittedly, there were occasions of brief terror as I maneuvered the unfamiliar right and left turns of the city's crowded streets. But the giddy feeling I had driving his little sports car between Baltimore and Washington more than compensated for those terrifying moments. Perhaps if Paul had had more time for me we may have developed a deeper relationship—he was certainly one of the nicest doctors I had met at Hopkins. By the time I left JHH, I had had many unique experiences, and driving Paul's car was one of them. I had also made two life long friends, Jack and Marilyn Mandler, he a surgeon and she a nurse, both of whom had been trained at Johns Hopkins.

As our second assignment at the University of Colorado did not start until the beginning of January 1962, Pam and I had three weeks of free time for further travel. We decided to drive down the east coast to Miami, then on to New Orleans, and from there into Mexico. As we said our goodbyes to our

Baltimore friends, the first snowflakes of winter began to softly fall around us. This was the first time either of us had ever known the magic of snow falling on city streets. The only snow I had ever seen had been on a ski trip to Mt. Kosciuszko in the Australian Alps. We would have a very different experience just three weeks later in Denver.

To save money we had contracted to drive a car from Baltimore to Miami, the owner of the car oblivious to our U.S. driving inexperience. In traveling down the coast of the southern states, we were frequently shocked by seeing areas of extreme poverty, as well as rest areas with signs for drinking water designated for "whites only" or for "coloreds only." At the time we didn't know it, but American cities were on the verge of many violent outbreaks of racial rioting, including Baltimore in 1968.

We thoroughly enjoyed the sun and balmy weather, and were especially impressed by the beautiful and stately homes of Charleston, South Carolina, and Savannah, Georgia, with only a vague awareness of their place in the history of the American Civil War. When we arrived in Miami and had safely delivered the car, we agreed that we didn't really like Miami and headed straight for New Orleans, a city we knew we were going to love. Once there we spent most of our time in the French Quarter, absorbing the vitality and colorful lifestyle all around us. On Bourbon Street we thoroughly enjoyed the sounds of jazz coming from every store and bar. I fell in love with the music of Jelly Roll Morton and bought one of his records. I also fell back into old habits and bought Beethoven's *Fifth Symphony*. After three days or so, as much as we loved New Orleans, Mexico was beckoning.

As we boarded a bus bound for Mexico City, we were slightly disconcerted at the obvious overcrowding of the bus, especially the sight of some of the passengers carrying chickens, piglets, and other small animals tucked into their laps. Our discomfort soon bordered on terror as the driver continually turned to talk to the passengers behind him. This was as he steered the bus around sharp corners on narrow roads through the mountains. After looking out the window and seeing the precipitous drop—and no guard rails—I stopped looking. I decided I would take a fatalistic approach: we may get there, and then again, we may not. Countless hours later, we arrived in Mexico City, none the worse for our experience, other than being emotionally exhausted. However, perhaps unfairly, I have never fully trusted any Mexican transportation since.

Mexico City was *huge*. Perhaps because it was so noisy, with the people speaking Spanish (a language we did not know) all around us, and the street traffic so chaotic, it seemed much bigger than any city in which I had ever been. To communicate I used my rudimentary knowledge of Italian. This I had learned in Australia to help me speak with Italian immigrant patients. Using what I hoped was a Spanish pronunciation of my Italian, to some degree, seemed to work. For the first couple of days, Pam and I went to regular restaurants to eat. When we realized this was fast depleting our money, we began eating day old-bread and bought our food from street carts. We were lucky—we didn't get the "gringo" illness, and this also enabled us to melt more readily into the local scene. We went to some open markets to buy food and a few little souvenirs, and explored many of the incredibly beautiful Catholic churches. These churches, with their glorious stained glass windows, richly ornamented statues, and gold objects, contrasted sharply with the many street children who continually approached us asking for money. We quickly learned, as hard as it was, to not give any money, as this only resulted in many more children gathering around us.

On our way to our main destination, Acapulco on Mexico's Pacific coast, we visited two towns that I particularly remember because of their charm and beauty, Cuernavaca and Taxco. Beautiful Cuernavaca was close to Mexico City and the first place we visited. Our senses were filled by the sight of the hills covered with brightly colored flowers, and the lovely old colonial buildings. There were many town squares, and Pam and I enjoyed sitting under the trees of a bougainvillea-covered plaza and watching people go by. The locals called Cuernavaca the "City of Eternal Spring" because of its great year-round weather.

Taxco, surrounded by mountains, green hills, and valleys, was about 100 miles southwest of Mexico City. I fell in love with it the minute we arrived and admired its white stucco buildings with red roof tiles perched on steeply sloping hills, its winding cobbled streets, lovely old churches, and charming small plazas. In the main plaza was the pride of the people of Taxco, a beautiful Baroque-style cathedral with rose-colored twin towers. Silver shops lined the streets of this former silver mining town, offering high-quality silver jewelry and goods. Pam and I spent many hours watching and mixing with the locals as well as with fellow visitors, enjoying lots of activity and laughter all around us. At the time, I thought if it ever became possible, I would love to live in this beautiful city.

Our final destination was Acapulco on Mexico's Pacific coast, a beach town backed by the Sierra Madre del Sur mountains. We checked into a modest resort, with a quietly happy and relaxed setting of mostly Mexican families. The pleasantly warm weather made the cold showers perfectly fine after a day of swimming at the beach, and our accommodations were simple and clean. Our free breakfast consisted of unlimited amounts of fruit juice, bowls of many varieties of fruit, my favorite being mango, and loaves of bread and bowls of cereal. Pam and I made a point of filling up on breakfast food, as we usually didn't eat again until the evening. On New Year's Eve, our last night in Mexico, we splurged with most of our remaining money and ate at a good restaurant. At the table next to us we recognized the beautiful, rich and famous actress Hedi Lamar. We were aware that she had recently been charged with stealing inexpensive items from stores, which of course made no sense given her wealth. Pam and I agreed that she may have been suffering from a condition called *kleptomania,* or compulsive stealing, and we felt sympathy for her.

A highlight of the evening was watching professional divers plunge down a hundred feet from the cliff, *La Quebrada,* into the sea below. They had to time their dives exactly right so that the waves that rolled in and out of the cove came back in and covered the rocks at the moment they hit the water. Before each person dived, he knelt in prayer, asking his God to protect him. It was breathtaking to watch. I couldn't think of a more frightening way to earn a living as these men did, risking their lives several times every day and night!

The next day Pam and I began our journey back to the United States. We had thoroughly enjoyed traveling in Mexico, a country rich in history and cultural diversity, a land of friendly people, of beauty, of wealth, and of abject poverty. In one week we would be starting on our new assignment at the University of Colorado. We were both excited and slightly apprehensive imagining the challenges that lay ahead.

As we arrived in Denver we were greeted by a severe snowstorm, which resulted in many traffic accidents, and in some cases, the closing off of some city streets. The beauty of our first snowstorm captivated us, my only concern being that I had no boots in which to navigate the snow-filled streets. I did not know until meeting him six months later that my future husband, Jack Hussey, had arrived in Denver that same weekend. He recounted that his difficulty had been in navigating Denver's streets in his small car, a Karmann Ghia. At one point strangers helped push him out of a deep snow drift so he could continue on his way. As I have since come to believe, life is filled with such coincidences!

Our assignment at the University of Colorado was for 18 months at the Colorado General Hospital. Pam was assigned to an adult medical unit, and I was assigned to a pediatric unit with patients aged from babies to two years. The senior medical supervisors on my unit were Drs. Henry Kempe and Henry Silver. Dr. Kempe's medical focus and research were in the elimination of worldwide smallpox and the health and safety of children. Dr. Silver's focus was diabetes. Dr. Kempe later received two nominations for the Nobel Prize. The first was for his work in developing a safer smallpox vaccine, which helped in the worldwide elimination of smallpox. The second nomination was for his contribution to the prevention and treatment of child abuse.

I enjoyed working with infants again. Dr. Kempe, himself a father of six daughters, had a hard and fast rule on behalf of the babies, based on studies of psychologists Rene Spitz, John Bowles, and others. All visitors, regardless of their status or reason for being there, were required to put a gown over their street clothes, sit in a rocking chair, and give a baby at least half an hour of cuddling. This was to counter the possible negative effects, such as emotional and cognitive deprivation, due to the baby's abrupt loss of contact with its primary attachment figure, usually the mother.

One day, an eighteen-month-old little girl was admitted to the unit. Her body was covered in bruises and cigarette burns. X-rays revealed that she had several bone fractures, some old, some more recent. At first Elizabeth was withdrawn and apathetic. However, after a few weeks, she began to make eye contact and smile in response to the nurses' and doctors' attentions. By the time she had been with us for several weeks, we all had become extremely fond of her. Finally, her body was healed, and she was ready to be discharged. Dr. Kempe attempted to obtain a court order to get an alternative living situation for her, but was unsuccessful, and she had to be returned to her biological family. Several weeks later, she was re-admitted to our unit, once again covered in bruises and with a new bone fracture. Dr. Kempe immediately applied for and obtained a court order preventing her from being returned to her family. Child abuse was something he had long been aware of. That same year, Drs. Kempe and Brandt Steele published a paper, "The Battered Child Syndrome," which led to the identification and recognition by the medical community of child abuse, for which Dr. Kempe received his second Nobel Prize nomination. Looking back, I realized with shock that I'd seen battered babies before. None of us had recognized it as parental abuse at the time.

In July 1962, I transferred to the research unit, where the patients were both children and adults. One of the patients I established a close relationship with while there was a twelve-year-old Ute Indian girl, Mary Jane. She was there as part of a study related to her diabetic condition. A quiet, modest girl, typical of her Native American culture, she showed much maturity for her age. I enjoyed discussing her thoughts and concerns with her. As a farewell gift she made me a small painted sculpture of an Indian woman carrying a baby on her back, which I was honored to accept and which I still have.

Another child whom I became emotionally attached to was Royal, a twelve-year-old African American boy, who was undergoing several weeks of preparation prior to having a kidney transplant. Every day I enjoyed watching *Captain Kangaroo* on TV with this boy, who impressed me with his calm attitude toward his upcoming surgery. His surgeon, Dr.Tom Starzl, was one of the pioneers of this surgery in the U.S., and later internationally known for pioneering liver transplants. In those days many patients did not survive long after their transplants due to unexpected complications. Happily, Royal's surgery was successful. This was mostly due to the fact that his mother donated one of her kidneys, which was a perfect match for Royal. I was able to follow his progress for more than twenty years, and the last I heard of him I was pleased to learn that he was doing well.

In September Jack Hussey returned from a summer spent working down south, and entered his first year of medical school at the University of Colorado. I had met him briefly the previous June, on a blind date set up by my roommate, Liz Bachlund. On his return to Colorado, our relationship grew serious. Jack was physically attractive, with an athletic build, sun-bleached blond hair, and startlingly blue eyes. He had an easy-going manner, which I liked. In December he invited me to travel to Savanna, Illinois to meet his parents. His father, Lemuel, a physician, had been the town's doctor for about thirty years at that time, and his mother, Berenice, was a retired school music teacher. I felt welcomed by them, and was happy to also meet his brother, David, already a doctor, and his sister, Kathleen, who was married to a Marine fighting in Vietnam.

On December 22, 1962, Jack asked me to marry him, and I accepted, so Christmas that year was an especially happy one. On February 22, 1963, Jack and I were married. I knew this was going to create serious problems for me, as at the completion of my nursing contract under the sponsorship of the American Nurses Association, I was required to return to Australia for two years.

I was not wrong. I began receiving regular warnings, about every six weeks, of my impending deportation, and although my visa was not due to expire until August 1, 1963, the Department of Immigration took my passport. Although I was married to an American citizen, I was considered an illegal alien. Jack's father was not only Savanna's doctor, but was also the Coroner for Cook County, Illinois, and a Republican with many influential friends in Congress. One of them was the highly regarded and politically powerful Senate Minority Leader Everett Dirksen, Illinois. When Jack's father told him of my problem, Senator Dirksen wrote to me of his interest and personal involvement on my behalf. Shortly thereafter, on June 18, 1963, Illinois Representative John Anderson introduced Bill HR7128, and on July 15, 1963 Colorado Senator Peter Dominick introduced Bill S1874 in my name, requesting a waiver of my deportation. From time to time I received encouraging and supporting letters from one or another of the three congressmen, sometimes including printed excerpts from the *Congressional Record* discussing my situation.

Meanwhile, once I had completed my contract in June 1963, I was no longer sponsored as a nurse by the American Nurses Association. This meant that I could no longer work as a nurse in the U.S. Happily, despite my rusty shorthand and typing skills, I applied for and was hired as secretary to the director of the Department of Physical Rehabilitation, Dr. Harold Dinken, at a local Denver hospital.

Dr. Dinken was a great boss, and he was also great friends with Isaac Stern. A highlight of my time working there was the day Mr. Stern came to visit him, and Dr. Dinken called me in to meet him. He boasted that his Australian secretary made a great cup of tea, and requested that I do so for his friend. Unfortunately, I was so bedazzled by meeting this great violinist, I brewed a terrible cup of tea. As he took his first sip, his facial expression momentarily changed, and then, gentleman that he was, he smiled and thanked me. Only later did I realize that, on hearing bubbling sounds emerge from the kettle, I had mistakenly believed the water had boiled. So the "tea" I served him had been a tasteless and cold cup of colored water!

A terrible tragedy occurred on November 22, 1963 when President John F. Kennedy was assassinated. I had only been in the U.S. a little over two years, but I felt as shocked and bereaved as if I had lived there forever. It was my first real awareness of the underlying level of hostility and violence in what was to become my adopted country.

While working for Dr. Dinken, I became pregnant, with my baby due in November 1964. Due to the quaint American custom of not allowing a working person to be obviously pregnant, I was required to resign from my job in September 1964.

November 6, 1964: A sunny, late fall afternoon. I was three days overdue as I sat chatting in the garden of our Denver home with Jack's parents, visiting from Savanna. As we sat surrounded by songbirds and late autumn flowers, I realized that I had begun to have regular, increasingly strong contractions. Anxious to call Jack, I discovered that the back door was locked. Hurrying to the front of the house, I found that that door was also locked. Then I noticed that the upstairs bedroom window was open. A ladder would solve the problem: Helpfully, Lemuel brought the ladder from the garage and leaned it up against the window. Then he looked expectantly at me. Clearly he did not consider Berenice or himself able to climb the ladder. So I hauled my enlarged abdomen up the ladder, over the windowsill and down into the bedroom. Grabbing my hospital-ready suitcase, I headed downstairs, and opened the front door to my waiting in-laws. Jack was called, and soon arrived from where he was working on the surgical ward at Colorado General Hospital.

Once admitted to the hospital's maternity ward, I began using the breathing techniques of the Lamaze method. This I had recently learned from the book *Thank You, Dr. Lamaze*. Somewhat to my surprise, this technique enabled me to control and have a drug- and pain-free labor. Jack had gone downstairs with my obstetrician, Dr. Richard Harvey, for a snack, and while they were gone, my labor progressed rapidly. A phone call beckoned Jack back to my room in time to be told that I was fully dilated and ready to be moved to the delivery room. At 2.24 a.m. November 7, 1964, Matthew David Hussey was born.

Two days after Matt's birth, a news reporter appeared asking permission to write a feature about Matt and me for her paper. Before Matt's birth, I had requested and been given "rooming in," a new concept at the time. This meant that Matt stayed with me after he was born, instead of going to the nursery as was the usual custom. The two of us were a front page news feature, including a picture, in the *Rocky Mountain News*. A few months later, we would again be in the news, this time in the other daily newspaper, *The Denver Post*, again with a picture, this time reporting on my ongoing immigration problems. The article and picture were relayed to Adelaide's daily newspaper, *The News*, and were featured in the social news section, much to the surprise of my Adelaide family and friends.

Matt was an easy-going baby, who ate and slept well right from the start, with a happy personality, and whose coos and twinkly eyes delighted us all. Lemuel and Berenice were thrilled with their first grandchild. Lemuel, who in his long service had delivered literally thousands of babies over three generations, loved to snuggle and kiss Matt, who would hug him back and nestle his face into Lemuel's shoulder. One of Jack's favorite activities was holding Matt firmly in his grasp, and then swinging him way up into the air above him, letting go, then catching him as he descended, to Matt's delight and my barely concealed fear! Jack and I, both fairly good skiers, would take him to various ski resorts in the Colorado Rockies, and because of Matt's sunny nature, had no hesitation in leaving him in the child care provided.

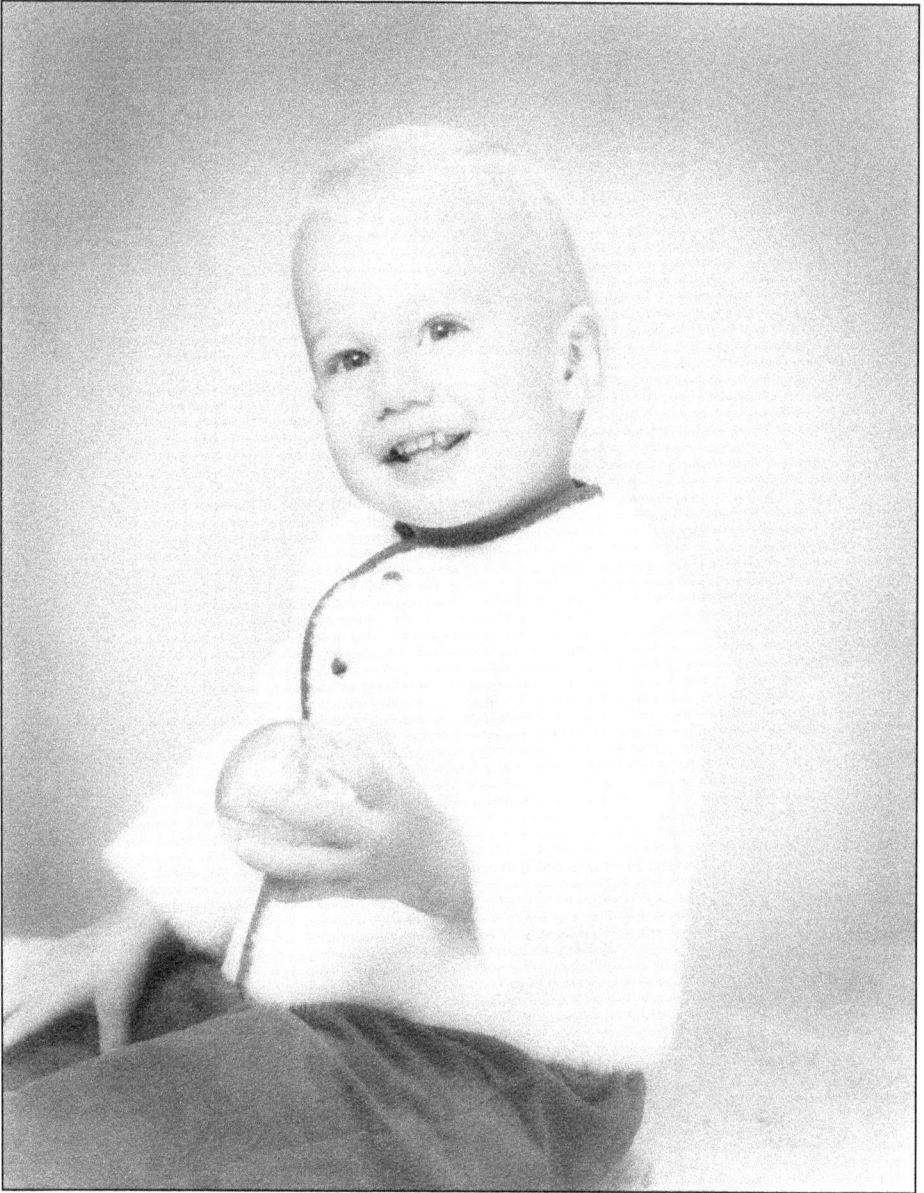

Baby Matt, 1965

On our long road trips from Denver to Jack's parents' home in Illinois, Matt would usually play and sleep in the back seat of our little Karmann Ghia car. However, on one of these trips, he was cutting a tooth, and when we stopped for the night at a motel in Nebraska, he began fussing and crying. Nothing we did could settle him, so Jack decided a ride in the Ghia would do the trick. So off they went, and I relaxed and began getting ready for sleep, expecting Jack would soon be back. Finally, more than an hour later, he returned with a bizarre story. Driving around the nearby streets, as expected, had quickly lulled Matt to sleep, and Jack began heading back to the motel. Suddenly, the night air was split with the sound of sirens, and he found himself surrounded by the flashing lights of several police cars. Ordered in no uncertain terms to get out of the car, a frightened Jack did so carefully. What followed turned out to be a case of mistaken identity. Apparently our little car, traveling the dark quiet streets of this Nebraska town, had matched the description of a car at the scene of an area bank robbery. The man they were seeking had murdered three people by shooting them in the back of their heads. It took the police no more than a few minutes of questioning, reinforced by the evidence of a sleeping baby in the back of the car, to apologize and let Jack go, shaken, but none the worse for his experience. Matt slept through it all, unaware of the drama that had just unfolded around him in the dark of the night.

At seven months, Matt began to walk independently, and before he was one year old, he was running everywhere. Tim, the eleven-year-old boy next door, became a regular visitor, fascinated with this happy little boy who was so responsive to any game Tim conjured up for them to play together. A favorite activity of Matt's was to sit on a three-wheeler bike and steer it around the garden paths while Tim pushed him as fast as possible.

On May 4, 1966, after receiving notices of my impending deportation every six weeks or so for the previous three years, Jack and I were excited and immensely relieved to receive a letter from John Clingan, director of the Department of Immigration in Denver, informing me that I had been granted a waiver of the requirement to return to Australia for two years. At this point, I took and passed the American Nurses' Association exams, qualifying me to work as an RN in the United States. I immediately began the formal procedure requesting permanent resident status. This "declaration of intent" turned into a three-year process before I was eligible to apply for U.S. citizenship. I was declared a naturalized U.S. citizen by Wisconsin Governor Jim Doyle on May 25, 1973.

In May 1966, Jack graduated from the University of Colorado. His next assignment would start on June 29 as an intern at Evanston Hospital, affiliated with Northwestern University, in Chicago. In late June we rented a small U-Haul trailer and packed it with our boxes, cartons, bikes, and Matt's toys and rocking horse. After saying farewell to everyone, including our medical school friends, many of whom we never saw again, we set out for the Midwest. With eighteen-month-old Matt we were heading for what was to be an entirely new way of life.

Chapter 4

June 28, 1966.

Most interns starting their one-year postgraduate training at Evanston Hospital were, like us, married with one or more children. We were all assigned apartments of varying sizes on the hospital grounds. As Jack and I had only one child, our apartment had two bedrooms. Although there was no formal meeting room, the interns' spouses (all women, of course, in those days of male-dominated medicine) quickly became acquainted with each other. On sunny days we gathered on the lawn separating us from the hospital and watched our children playing as we chatted with each other. Although Matt was a quiet child, he quickly became bonded in friendship with a little girl, Bethany. Her mother, Anne, and I delighted in watching these two little ones play so happily together. Soon we became good friends, too.

On the morning of July 14, 1966, our small community was horrified to read in the newspaper of the murder during the night of eight nurses from the South Chicago Community Hospital. Apparently the murderer, later identified as Richard Speck, had tied up all eight nurses at gunpoint and methodically raped and killed each nurse one by one. A ninth nurse had managed to hide under a bed and escaped notice. After he left, people heard her screams and discovered the grisly scene. This was only two weeks after we had arrived in Evanston, a northern suburb of Chicago. This reinforced my belief that Chicago, home of gangsters, was a dangerous city indeed.

This unspeakable tragedy preyed on my mind, and I felt afraid at night whenever I was alone with Matt. This was often, as when Jack was on duty the phone on our kitchen wall would summon him to the hospital several times in the night. Although I begged him to lock the door every time he left, my pleas went unanswered. Many were the times I would force myself awake and out of bed to check the door. It was always unlocked. This was unmistakable evidence to me of Jack's disregard for my safety and a clear indication of his limited love for me. It was the first significant crack in our relationship.

In 1966 it had been five years since I had left my birth country, intending to return two years later. Since my departure, my father had died unexpectedly on December 12, 1964, coincidentally on Jack's birthday, and only five weeks after Matt's birth. A week before Dad's death, I had felt an increasingly strong urge to make contact with him. Jack responded to my heightened emotions by urging me to call Australia. I did so, and spoke first with my mother, and then with my brother, David. Neither told me that Dad was dying, presumably in an effort to spare my feelings. Three days after my call, Dad died. I later learned that while going in and out of a semicomatose state, he had been calling my name. Given my immigration difficulties at the time, I was unable to travel to Australia. However, after receiving a waiver of deportation from the Department of Immigration on May 4, 1966, my passport was returned to me, and I was free to travel again. I decided the time had come for me to visit Australia.

In mid-August 1966, Matt, now 19 months old, and I set out on our trip. I had been so excited to be going, in anticipation of my family meeting him, that I had overlooked the fact that as an American, Matt needed a visa to enter Australia. On arriving in San Francisco, the authorities informed me of my oversight. At a late hour of that night, the U.S. consul was awakened and his presence urgently requested at the airport. He responded quickly, a diplomatic man whose agreeable manner helped allay the embarrassment I was feeling. Matt was given the necessary documentation, and we were on our way.

It was not an easy trip. It took about twenty hours to cross the Pacific, during which time Matt not only did not sleep, but persisted in running up and down the aisle much of the time. Two young soldiers in the seats behind us added fuel to his already overexcited state. After climbing up on his seat to peek at them, with their encouragement, he began trying out some new words…"muck, duck,…." Of course, he soon found the word they were hoping for! In response to their delighted laughter, Matt enunciated what had suddenly become his favorite word for what seemed like a very long time. Eventually, though, he began to slow down, and about an hour out of Sydney, he fell into an exhausted sleep. The man seated next to me looked at my innocent little child and muttered, "Thank God!."

As we came out of Customs, we were met by the waving arms and big smiles of my friends, Ian and Ros Craig. Ian, renowned in the wide world of British Commonwealth cricket for having been Australia's youngest test cricket captain ever, had been a close friend of mine for the two years prior to my leaving Australia in 1961. At that time, I had introduced him to Ros, a nursing buddy of mine, who for some years had admired him from afar. At the time that I had asked Ian to meet Ros, his rueful response had been, "Are you trying to get rid of me?" I truthfully denied this, as no such thought had occurred to me. As it transpired, the attraction between them was instant and electric. Within a year of my departure, they had married in a wedding that, given Ian's status in the cricket world, had been covered internationally. Happily, Ian, Ros, and I remained good friends, and on this trip and all subsequent trips, we alays looked forward to our time together en route to my family in Adelaide. After four days of Sydney time with Ian and Ros, Matt and I were on the plane to Adelaide.

It was wonderful to be with my family again and to spend time with my friends. However, I was concerned knowing that a rubella (German measles) epidemic was raging in Australia, and I possibly was in early pregnancy. On arriving at the Adelaide airport I was met by my brother and his family and spent the ride to his home snuggled up to one of his daughters, Bronwyn. One week later, David called to tell me that Bronwyn had become ill with German measles. In 1966 the rubella vaccine had yet to be developed. Especially in early pregnancy, rubella was known to cause serious birth defects, including heart, eye, and hearing problems, as well as death. Although not knowing for sure if I was pregnant, my doctor gave me an injection of gamma globulin, antibodies that would boost my immune system and help protect my fetus against the rubella virus.

I continued to spend time with family and friends, including enjoying picnics, beach parties, and camping trips into the Flinders Ranges north of Adelaide. Sleeping under the star-filled skies of the Outback, breathing in the delicious aroma of the eucalyptus trees, my heart rejoiced. And then in early October, a day after enjoying an afternoon at a children's birthday party, I had a call from one of the mothers—her daughter had become ill with German measles. By this time, I knew I was pregnant. Once again, I was given an injection of gamma globulin, and I tried my best to not worry about my pregnancy.

This was a time when the war in Vietnam was increasing in intensity under the Johnson administration. The Australian military had already sent troops to join the United States in fighting the war, a cause of much controversy in Australia. Heated discussions would often arise in social gatherings. Although

I personally held strong antiwar beliefs, I felt caught between loyalty to the United States even as I mostly shared the opinions of my Australian friends, and so I frequently found these situations difficult to navigate. However, once back in the U.S. and as the war intensified, I became actively involved in U.S. antiwar activities. I attended many antiwar rallies and made my home available for antiwar meetings.

All too soon it was time for Matt and me to return to the United States. My brother David drove Matt and me to the Adelaide airport, with his wife Peg, Mummy, and my sister Mary along to wave goodbye. As I looked back one last time at them before walking down the long passage to the waiting plane, I felt a deep sense of sadness. I had no idea when I would be able to return to my beloved Australia.

Matt and I flew from Adelaide to Sydney to spend two more days with Ian and Ros Craig, before they drove us to the airport. Soon after taking off from Sydney, even as I caught my last glimpse of the Sydney Harbor Bridge and shoreline, I became aware that something was wrong with Matt. He had begun to whimper, and soon he was crying fitfully, his little body becoming restless and increasingly warm to the touch. As he closed his eyes, and slumped down in my arms, it was clear that he was ill. Observing this, a stewardess came to my side and questioned me as to what could be wrong with him. I pleaded ignorance, although secretly worried: could it be German measles? After observing Matt a few more moments, she left me to consult with the pilot. On her return, she asked me to consider the pilot's proposal: that he redirect our flight north to Brisbane, in the state of Queensland, so I could get medical attention for Matt. All I could think of was that I knew no one in Queensland, that I did not want to be left there with a sick child, and that I needed to get back home. I refused the offer. She did not give up, continuing to go back and forth between me and the pilot. Each time she returned, she repeated the pilot's willingness to turn back and fly to Brisbane. Each time, I refused. Finally, she came back to me, and said, "We are at the point of no return. We must keep going now." I acknowledged this fact, thanked her for her concern, and prepared myself for what lay ahead. By this time, the passengers near me had moved as far back as possible into empty seats, clearly as concerned for their safety as I was for what was wrong with my little boy.

A few hours later, we landed in Honolulu, and went through what felt like a lengthy process through Customs. Mercifully, by this time Matt had settled down, and seemed almost his usual self. We continued to San Francisco and, after changing planes, some five hours later we landed in Chicago and there was Jack! He was so excited to see us that as his arms reached out, he dropped our much-prized Super 8 movie camera. Until then this camera had recorded Matt's every move. Although it was not broken, no recording was made that day of Matt's return from his first big adventure. Exhausted, and enormously relieved to relinquish my maternal responsibility, I handed Matt to Jack. As soon as I was in our car, I surrendered to sleep on the drive home. Two days later, Matt came down with German measles.

I was still in the first trimester of my pregnancy, and now I was very scared, for I knew what this could mean for our unborn child. Jack's father consulted with a medical colleague, who was knowledgeable about rubella-affected babies. I consulted with several medical people in Australia who had similar experiences with rubella in early pregnancies. Everyone strongly advised me to have an abortion, which although not legal at the time, I was assured could be made possible under the circumstances. The only person who did not suggest I have an abortion was Jack. He said, "Whatever you decide, I will support you." I was very grateful to him for this. Because I felt certain that our unborn child was meant to be, I decided to continue my pregnancy. At this point, my blood tested positive for the rubella virus, although I showed no clinical signs of having contracted it. What followed for us were six months of worry.

Shortly after I arrived home from Australia, Jack told me that he had never applied for a surgical residency, and so he had no idea what he was going to do once he finished his internship in June. This was a major oversight! My organizational skills clicked into place! After several days (or was it weeks) of scouring medical journals and hospital advertisements, our efforts paid off. A surgical residency position at the highly esteemed University of Wisconsin had suddenly opened up. This was unusual at such a late date, and the medical staff were requesting anyone interested to apply for the position as soon as possible. Jack immediately did so. On an overcast, cold winter day in early December, Jack, Matt, and I set out in our little Karmann Ghia for Madison, a city I had barely heard of and of which I knew nothing except that it was the capital of Wisconsin, where there were lots of cows.

At the hospital, Jack was met by a smartly dressed doctor, and after brief introductions, the two of them disappeared behind the door of a nearby hallway. Fortunately, Matt was his usual happy self, and the two of us entertained each other for the next two hours or so until Jack reappeared, with a big smile on his face. Perhaps as a measure of their desperation, after being interviewed by three physicians, he had been hired on the spot. We had a plan!

After a hasty meal, we began our journey back to Evanston. About an hour out from Madison, our little car suddenly slowed down and stopped. By now, it was pitch black on a country road, with no other vehicles in sight. Jack bundled up Matt and me in a blanket, locked us in the car, and set out for a built-up area we had passed a few minutes earlier. My memory of what happened after that is murky. I know Jack came back with a tow truck, and after hitching up the Ghia, had the driver take Matt and me to an Amtrak railway station. Presumably this was an informed decision by Jack, because before too long, a train came, and Matt and I climbed on board. Eventually we arrived in Chicago. Guided by intuition, as I had no knowledge of Chicago railways, we boarded a train for Evanston, arriving there at some very late hour. I have no recollection as to how we made it to our apartment (there were no cellphones in those days) but we did, just as Matt, who had been stoic throughout this adventure, melted down and began sobbing. Holding him close, and offering him soothing words, together we collapsed into exhausted sleep. Many hours later we awoke to a new day. I have no idea how Jack solved his end of the problem...but both he and the Ghia turned up sometime later. We had survived a challenging situation, but we were home, safe and sound. What's more, Jack had a contract for his surgical training for the next four or five years at the renowned and well respected University of Wisconsin.

Our December adventure was more than matched by what the next month had in store for us. On Thursday, January 26, 1967, (coincidentally the date celebrated as Australia Day 9,000 miles from me) Chicago suffered the worst blizzard in its known history. The forecast had been for about 4 inches of snow, but it just kept coming. By the end of Friday, 23 inches had fallen. Chicago ground to a halt. Airports shut down, cars and buses were abandoned in the street, public transportation stopped, and businesses closed. The few people on the Chicago streets were either walking or skiing to their destinations. The unaccustomed quietness cast a feeling of peacefulness over the city. A spirit of camaraderie took over as strangers began talking to each other and reached out to help those in distress. Expectant mothers were taken to hospitals by sled or snow plow. Area hospital staff already on duty (including Jack) stayed on duty, because no one could get to or from work.

In our Evanston community, schools were closed, and the children were having a wonderful time making snowmen and digging caves and castles into the huge mounds of snow all around us. Those who had plenty of food shared it with those who had not gone shopping before the storm. Inspired by this sense of community, I began to bake small loaves of whole wheat bread, ready to share with others. Friends and neighbors soon began coming to my door, responding to the delicious aroma spreading throughout the building. It felt great, even so briefly, to feel I was contributing with "the staff of life."

Slowly the months of my pregnancy passed. No matter what I was doing throughout that winter and spring, at the back of my mind was the persistent thought: How was my baby? In those days, amniocentesis and ultrasound had not been developed. Until a baby was born, not much could be known. Finally, the signs of early labor began. Jack came to my side quickly and called his mother to come and get Matt. She and a close friend arrived from Savanna in record time, about three hours later. I kissed Matt goodbye, and as they drove away, Jack and I walked across the lawn to the hospital. Because of my positive rubella titer, I was considered potentially infectious. Rather than the obstetric ward, I was admitted to the infectious disease ward. My attending doctor was Randy, a friend of Jack's, who was in his last year of residency in obstetrics at Evanston Hospital. After a relatively easy ninety minutes of labor, Stephen Bourne Hussey entered the world on May 12, 1967 at 4.56 p.m. Moments later, as Randy was focusing on my needs, I observed Steve's color changing from pink to a shade of blue. "What is wrong with my baby?" I shouted in panic. Randy looked down, and instantly snatched Steve up in his arms. As he ran out the door, my last view was of him "mouth to mouthing" Steve. Jack and I waited several long minutes in anxious near silence until Randy returned. He told two very relieved people that after suctioning mucus out of Steve's mouth, he had quickly "pinked up." Before Randy had left with Steve, Jack and I had both glimpsed the mucus around his mouth and had feared he was choking because of a cleft palate, a not-unusual complication of a rubella-affected baby.

Shortly after these moments of drama, as I prepared myself to take Steve from the nurse holding him near my bedside, I spoke. To our surprise, this baby, little more than an hour old, responded to my voice by shakily turning his bobbing head on its fragile neck toward the direction of my voice. He knew me! Yes! He was meant to be!

All subsequent tests proved to be normal, but my stay in the infectious disease ward was difficult for me. The nurses had relatively little understanding of the needs of a new mother, and restricted to my room, which had only a small sink, I longed for a refreshing shower. Because Steve had been "mouth-to-mouthed" by Randy, he was awakened every few hours, usually right after I had settled him, for an antibiotic injection. This was to protect him from developing any infection from his contact with Randy. This was upsetting for me, but a small price to pay for maintaining my baby's health. Finally, exhausted from lack of sleep, I convinced Jack to arrange for me to

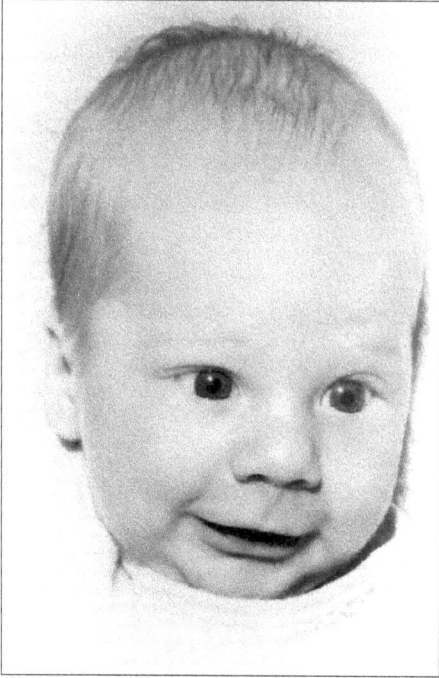

Baby Steve, 3 days old, 1967

go home earlier than usual. The walk across the lawn to our apartment was a joyous one; a long, hot shower and the comfort of home welcomed me. We had a healthy baby boy! A huge weight was lifted from our shoulders.

In mid-June 1967, Jack's internship was over. We packed our few possessions into a U-Haul, which Jack drove, and our little boys into the Karmann Ghia, which I drove, and left for Jack's surgical residency in Madison. Our new home was a little box house we rented on Craig Avenue on the west side of Madison. There were many other people like us, just starting their careers, several of whom became good friends. We would go to each of our little box houses to share meals, to play cards, and with one friend, I would play chess. Ted considered himself a good chess player. However, it secretly amused me to watch Ted's respirations increase and sweat begin to form on his brow on the occasions that it became apparent I was about to declare checkmate. Although I liked Ted, he was a man of his time, and he clearly hated to lose to a woman. Jack's and my two closest friends were Paris and Molly. Paris, from Iran, was a physician, and his wife, Molly, was an English-trained RN. I especially enjoyed Molly's English sense of humor, and the four of us shared many interests and outdoor activities over a decade of friendship.

Shortly after arriving in Madison I returned to my nursing career, caring for transplant patients at the University Hospital to help augment Jack's meager earnings as a first-year surgical resident. Jack earned extra dollars in his few hours off moonlighting locally in the emergency room of St. Mary's Hospital. Sometimes the only times we would see each other would be as our paths crossed when one of us was starting a shift and the other was returning home from the University Hospital.

Behind the houses on Craig Avenue stretched a lawn unencumbered by fencing. Over the next fifteen months, I would watch my children playing the length of this lawn with the many other children who called Craig Avenue home. Our house was at the end of the street at a cul de sac, with a tunnel which led under a raised area, emerging onto a main street at Knoche's, a small mom-and-pop grocery store. Sometimes I would go through the tunnel with Matt and baby Steve to buy some candy or an ice cream cone.

Early in March 1968, a few days before my birthday on the 12th, I found a little plant in a tiny pot hidden behind my radio. I realized that Matt, not much more than three years old, must have gone through the tunnel by himself and bought it with his few pennies for my birthday. So I kept it watered until the big day, and acted very surprised when he presented it to me. One year later, I received exactly the same present, which was truly a surprise this time. I asked him how he had decided to give me the very same present. He happily replied, "Because you were so happy with it on your last birthday." Both plants grew and survived for many years. They were always a happy memory of my little boy's thoughtful and loving gesture.

In October 1968, I resigned my position caring for transplant patients, as we were now expecting our third child, due in January 1969. Our little house on Craig Avenue could not easily accommodate a third child, so in November we bought a ranch-style house on Old Middleton Road in preparation for the big event. As I had been successful with my first two children to have short and pain-free labors, I was anxious to find an obstetrician sympathetic to my belief in the Lamaze technique. I was happy to find this person, Dr. William Kiekhofer, who supported me in managing my own labor.

Saturday, January 17, 1969 dawned a frigid day, with snow in the forecast. When I met Dr. Kiekhofer for my weekly checkup, he informed me that my cervix was already retracting significantly in preparation for the birth. As Jack was working, I was feeling apprehensive about what would probably be a quick labor with no one to get me to the hospital in time. Dr. Kiekhofer agreed to my urgent plea to be admitted into the hospital rather than going home. My next door neighbor and friend Josette agreed to care for Matt and Steve, and Jack was called to my bedside. Once Dr. Kiekhofer ruptured the "bag of waters" (membranes) of the placenta, there was no turning back. After two hours of no activity, with Jack several times saying, "I knew we shouldn't have done this," active labor began. I heard a doctor passing in the hallway and saying to someone, "There's a Lamonzer" in there. As busy as I was, I chuckled to myself. Three hours later, Katherine Anne entered the world at 5.50 p.m. I had my little girl. (On January 17, 2002, thirty-three years later to the day, Kate gave birth to her own little girl, Rebecca Katherine.)

Three days later, while Jack was moonlighting at St. Mary's Hospital, I was home alone with two active little boys and my new baby girl. As I sat

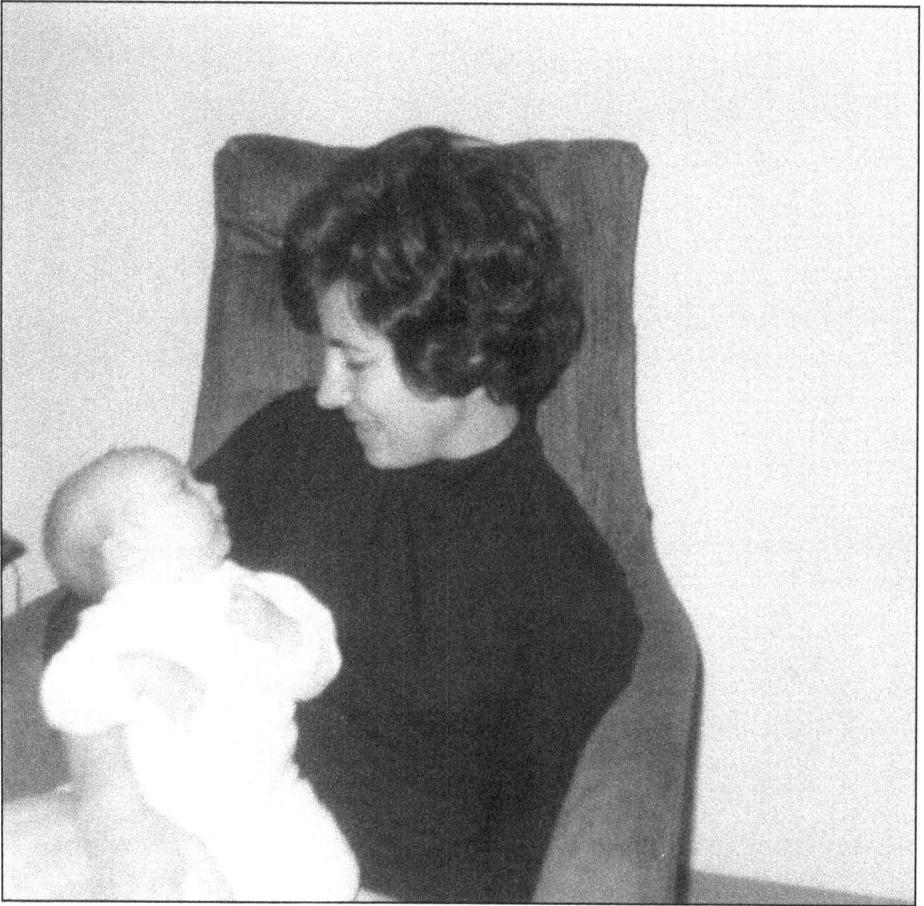

Kate at 2 months, March, 1969

in the rocking chair breastfeeding her, I speculated that within the next thirty minutes I could have Matt and Steve in their beds, and I could get some much-needed sleep. Then Matt tripped and hit his head on the edge of the brick fireplace, and I could see streaks of red in his blond hair. A brief look revealed a small cut, and I reassured him and myself that all was well. I returned to my fantasy that soon the boys would be in bed. Ten minutes later, Steve, running after Matt, slipped and fell against the sculptured leg of the cherrywood buffet. After a moment of startled silence, he ran screaming to me, blood streaming down his face. This time, the situation was clearly different. I could see the back of his throat through the large gap under his nose! Grabbing a towel, and wrapping it around his face, I frantically called my friend Sandy across the street. Mercifully, she was home and was instantly

Matt, Steve, and Katie, approximately 1970

at my front door. As I thrust little Katie into her arms, I saw reflected on her anxious face my own fears. Bundling both boys into the car, I somehow managed to arrive safely at the St. Mary's emergency room. As I did my best to calmly explain what had happened to the admitting physician, I sensed he was evaluating me. Was I not only an incompetent parent, with *two* injured

Matt, Katie, Steve, 1971

children, but possibly also an abusive one? Thankfully, Jack appeared on the scene, and the reassured doctor took Steve, quivering and crying, into the nearby surgery room. Someone else took Matt, who was returned to me a few minutes later with two stitches in his head.

Steve's screams wrenched my heart as they repaired his injured face. Some countless minutes later Jack emerged with Steve's shaking and exhausted little body. It had taken 32 stitches to repair his wound. As Jack's shift did not finish until morning, I was on my own with two upset little boys. Sandy came by with a very hungry Katie, and while I finished feeding her, Sandy led Matt and Steve down the hall to their beds. After helping them into their pajamas, she called me to come kiss them goodnight, even as they fell into exhausted sleep. Sandy had only been married a year or so, and I hoped that this night of drama did not deter her and her husband in any way from having children of their own.

And so began my life as the mother of three small children, which was much more difficult than having two. Dr. Kiekhofer had asked me if I would teach his patients the Lamaze method of childbirth. Flattered as I was in his confidence in me, I declined his offer. I anticipated challenging childcare times ahead, and as the wife of a doctor, I already knew to expect little shared parenting time from my overworked husband. However, Jack and I occasionally found time to play tennis on his days off. We also carved out time to drive in our large station wagon, newly acquired after Katie's birth, the nearly three hours from Madison to Illinois to spend time with Jack's parents in Savanna, a small town on the Mississippi River.

On our visits, I always enjoyed many hours of fishing the sloughs of the Mississippi River with Jack's father. Lemuel told me that his cronies would ask him after my fishing visits, "Where's the girl?" I also liked getting to know Jack's mother's friends, and listening to Berenice's many stories of this small Midwestern town. One day, as Lemuel and I drove down the main street, we passed a sign noting that the population of Savanna was 3,001 people. I asked him why that number never changed, and he joked, "Because every time a baby is born, a man leaves town."

I found time to continue my antiwar activities. In 1968 Lyndon Johnson, agonizing over the tens of thousands of Americans and hundreds of thousands of North Vietnamese dying in what was a truly terrible war, declared he would not run for a second term. As Americans learned later, Johnson, in a conversation with Senator Everett Dirksen, declared that Nixon, in a secret plot, had "committed treason," with which statement Dirksen had agreed. By conspiring with the South Vietnamese to sabotage Johnson's peace talks with the North Vietnamese, literally days before the election, Nixon won the presidency. At about this time, my fellow activists and I became aware that our phones were being tapped. Often we would hear strange clicking sounds during our conversations. This didn't intimidate us, although it probably should have, as we came to learn that Nixon had compiled a comprehensive "enemies list" of people like us. As a noncitizen who had had immigration difficulties in the recent past, I could have been especially vulnerable to the negative consequences of Nixon's antagonism. Kathleen, my sister-in-law, whose husband, Ron, was a Marine fighting in Vietnam, became openly hostile toward me because of my antiwar stance. This terrible war affected many families, as it did mine, and my relationship with Kathleen, which had never been particularly close, became strained.

My neighbors in the area of Old Middleton Road were friendly as I settled into my busy routine. We shared many activities with our children, including snow sledding, swimming in the neighbor's pool and tadpole collecting in the nearby ponds in the warmer months, and frequently sharing meals in each others' homes. Josette had three children, David, Marc, and Rachel, all of whom felt comfortable in their comings and goings between our homes. My

Dr. Lemuel and Berenice Hussey with kids, 1972

neighbors on the other side had four boys and a girl. Patti would sometimes babysit for me. The two youngest boys, Tommy and Bobby, became playmates of Matt and Steve. Bobby was a wild child, somewhat older than Steve, who influenced a similar tendency for wildness in Steve. When Steve was still in diapers, less than two years old, despite my padlocking the backyard gates, had escaped and run out onto Old Middleton Road. A neighbor alerted me that Steve was standing in the middle of the road, playing "chicken" with the cars. That was one time I pulled down his diaper and smacked his bottom!

At only three years old, Steve learned to ride a two-wheeler bike, and not a few were the times that I thought he was home when I would get a call from Wendy, the mother of a little girl, Alex, who Steve was fond of playing with, who lived three streets away from us. Wendy good naturedly would say, "Well, Jill, he turned up here again a few minutes ago," at the same time assuring me that all was well. Wendy was the only person I knew who frequently told me that if I ever needed to have respite from his challenging ways, she would be more than willing to keep him until I was recovered. Not even his grandparents ever made such an offer. They loved and welcomed Steve when he came to visit with his whole family, as long as he was under the care of his parents.

When Matt was four, he began attending a nearby Montessori school and flourished in the unique learning environment. He showed a natural aptitude for learning new things, both physically and academically. He was kind and patient with his competitive younger brother, who seemed compelled to try to do whatever Matt could do, even when it was sometimes unrealistic. Matt was joined at Montessori by Steve and Kate when they reached three. This allowed me more free time, and in 1972, when Kate was barely three, I found a part-time job as a typist.

When Steve was about four years old, apparently upset about something, he decided he would run away from home. My first awareness of this was a call from my friend Ruth's husband, Ed, to inform me that Steve had turned up at their home, which was about half a mile from ours. On arriving there, Steve had told them he was on his way to South America. He had put a banana, an apple, and a raincoat (he said he knew it rained a lot in South America) into a backpack before setting out. Apparently, he had become tired and called in to Ruth and Ed's for a rest. On collecting him from their home, I was careful to treat Steve's escapade with a respectful seriousness to avoid hurting his feelings. I never did discover the reason for his plan to run away.

In 1971, when Steve was about five, his playmate Bobby came running into my yard, yelling, "Mrs. Hussey, Steve is on the roof." I pulled open the kitchen sliding glass door just in time to see Steve jump off Bobby's upper-story roof. Expecting a terrible scene as I ran next door, I discovered that the two boys had built a large pile of autumn leaves for Steve to jump into. Presumably Bobby just wanted to scare me half to death! At about that same time, with a little help from Jack, Matt and Steve built a primitive treehouse in our front yard, with a rope ladder for access. This ladder was always retracted after they climbed into their house, and was only lowered for selective friends to join them for many happy hours of play. Occasionally, as Katie grew a little older, they allowed her to join them on certain occasions.

Katie was a confident, happy child, who fearlessly followed her brothers into whatever pursuits they undertook. An example of this comes to mind, when we were spending a summer day fishing off the pier at the University of Wisconsin's Memorial Union. Tired of fishing and ready for a new adventure, Matt started climbing a tree overhanging Lake Mendota. Steve quickly followed with Katie right behind. I held my breath as I watched them, afraid to react openly in case one of them fell, as they crawled to the end of a branch

Katie and Jack, 1973

hanging over the water. From there, while they perched on the swaying limb, they called out and cheerily waved to me as I did my best to appear calm and unconcerned. Katie's teachers at Montessori told me that they considered her physically well coordinated and suggested I involve her in gymnastics. This I did, and Katie spent several years in becoming a skilled gymnast. She also became a skilled athlete in several sports.

One memorable afternoon, as I entertained my friends for lunch, Steve came running through the kitchen on his way to the backyard. As he pulled the sliding glass door closed, it slammed on his pinky finger. With his screams piercing the air, he held up his hand, and I saw his finger hanging by what seemed to be only a thin strand of skin. My luncheon ended abruptly. Once again, an emergency room doctor saved the day, stitching Steve back together again. Fortunately, his finger remained healthy and served him well in the ensuing years, as he played the violin, and later still, as a veterinary surgeon.

About two years later, as I called my children to dinner, Matt came running in first, and slammed the door behind him. A very loud scream instantly followed, and Katie came into the room with blood pouring from her hand. Her pinky finger, like Steve's, was hanging by a strip of skin. Once again, after a frantic trip to the emergency room, a doctor successfully reattached it, with no further problem.

On a visit to Jack's parents with my children, I was pulled over by a sheriff, and cited for having an expired car registration, which apparently Jack had not updated. On keeping my court appearance some weeks later, I sat in the back of the courtroom with Matt, Steve, and Kate. On hearing my name called, I walked up the center aisle of the courtroom, and stood before the judge. I became aware of some snickering by people nearby, at the same moment as I heard Steve's voice singing "here comes the judge." I turned to see my three grinning children standing behind me. Another example of my children's naughty ways.

As if I didn't have enough to do caring for what my more diplomatic friends called my "lively children," in 1972 I began taking classes at Madison Area Technical College. Rediscovering that I loved learning, I was inspired to seek a college degree. In 1973 I transferred my newly earned credits into the University of Wisconsin undergraduate program, eventually graduating in January 1975 with a Bachelor of Science degree in Psychology. This was from Edgewood College, after I had transferred from the UW in order to be granted 33 credits from Edgewood in recognition of my nursing career. Immediately following this, I began to study for my Master's degree at the University of Wisconsin in Rehabilitation Counseling and Psychology.

Jack, Mummy, Katie, Steve, and self, August, 1974

On May 25, 1973 I was proud to become a naturalized citizen, with many others before Governor Jim Doyle, as a citizen of the United States. In doing so I was forced to relinquish my Australian citizenship. My expectation was that I would be living in the United States for the remainder of my life. I also believed I could not fully participate in the political and social scene without

Ruth and Jill, about 1974

being a citizen, and that overrode my sense of loss in no longer being a citizen of my birth country.

In June, 1973 my mother came to live with Jack and me and our children for a year. This proved to be a happy time, for which I am grateful. It gave us the opportunity to know each other as adults and as mothers, and for me to fully appreciate Mummy as the loving and selfless parent she had been to me in my growing-up years. Mummy and Jack also formed a mutually affectionate relationship. It was heartwarming for me to see how kind and thoughtful he was with her. Jack's parents invited Mummy to their home two or three times, as well as occasionally visiting us in Madison. My friend, Ruth Feige, whom I'd been close to since Kate was a baby, when our children had attended Montessori School together, had proven to be someone I counted on to help make my mother's stay comfortable. She would often drive Mummy to her pottery class, or to her activity group at a local church, or to an occasional appointment, as well as inviting us all to join her family and friends at small dinner parties. My mother always found time to make healthy after school snacks for the children, and obviously much enjoyed her role as grandmother. They in turn loved her, and her different ways of doing and saying things—especially her strong Australian accent. In later years I read entries in the diary she kept while she lived with us. I was impressed with her insightful impressions of her three American grandchildren. I sincerely believe it was one of the happiest periods of her life—and perhaps one of the best years that Jack and I shared also.

After Mummy returned to Australia in 1974, perhaps as a result of losing her calming influence on Jack and me, our marriage deteriorated, as it had been doing for a while. In the early years of our marriage, both of us in our twenties, Jack and I had been drawn to each other's physical attractiveness and interest in sports. New to America, with only a vague awareness of U.S. history and politics, we rarely discussed our personal ideology. With the escalation of the Vietnam War in the late 1960s, I began to recognize the differences in Jack's and my world view, more so as I became increasingly involved in antiwar activities. This was also the time of the rise of the women's movement, and I began to question and resist my traditional role as a married woman. Like many others at the time, I helped form what was known as a consciousness-raising group, a safe place for women to explore and understand the social changes exploding all around us. For several years, seven of us met weekly, opening our hearts and minds to each other in a way that we had never felt able to do before.

Over those years, I found myself increasingly out of step with Jack's ideals and values, as he did with mine. This gradually changed our expectations and acceptance of each other. Ultimately, neither of us was able to truly appreciate the other, and I found myself feeling increasingly alone and lonely within my marriage. Finally, in May 1976, I requested a separation from Jack. We had been living in a cold and unfriendly house in Cross Plains for about a year at that time. Jack moved out, and built his new home on a cliff outside of Cross Plains, and I moved into a house on Main Street in July 1976. On October 10, 1977 we were divorced, and a new life began for me as a single woman, at forty-one years of age.

Chapter 5

Following our separation in July 1976, I lived in a house on Main Street in Cross Plains. With the help of a sympathetic realtor, I bought the house on a one-year land contract. This meant no money down, then selling it back to the original owner at the same price at the end of the year. This worked well for me, giving me time to search for a permanent home. For that year Matthew, Steve, and Katie moved back and forth between my home and Jack's newly built home on a weekly schedule.

I loved my house on Main Street, with the front door's stained glass windows and a balcony looking out on the back yard. All the children enjoyed sleeping out there on warm summer nights, the small town's dark sky sparkling with stars. Never having lived in a two-story home, their new activities included climbing on the roof to survey Main Street and the surrounding countryside,and exploring the attic, occasionally finding forgotten objects of former owners. One day, Matt found a tarnished saxophone, and after unsuccessfully attempting to play it, relegated it as a decoration in the back garden. They all liked their teachers, Katie especially. When she happened to meet her teacher in a local store, Katie shyly said hello to her, overcome with the realization that she had a life other than being a teacher. Unlike their first school year in Cross Plains, while we were living on Highway P, living on Main Street meant they could walk to school every morning, often with one of their classmates. I too found myself enjoying small town life. One of my favorite spots to spend time was at the local garden store, swapping anecdotes with the young woman who owned it, as well as learning a lot about plants. Despite our marital troubles, I was heartened to see my children adjusting to the many changes in their lives and seeming to be happy.

One of the first things I learned in my new single state was to always have some kind of planned activity every weekend, with or without my children. This strategy helped counter a hovering sense of anxiety, fear, and depression to which I awoke many mornings. Since we had moved to Madison, Jack and my closest friends had been Paris and Molly Malek. At the time of our separation, Molly, holding eye contact with me with difficulty, said, "Paris and I are not able to continue as we were. We have to choose between you and Jack, and we choose Jack. I'm sorry." Jack's mother and sister made it clear that I was no longer considered a member of the Hussey family. Jack's father, who wanted to maintain contact with me, was informed of this by Berenice and Kathleen, and accepted their ruling. How I wished that my own family, my mother in particular, weren't 10,000 miles away!

I decided the time had come to return to the comfort and familiarity of Australia. So in early December 1976, I prepared for a two-month trip home, using Frequent Flier miles I had acquired since my 1966 trip with Matt. In discussing this with Jack, we agreed that Matt's and Steve's schooling would suffer from such a long break, so only Katie would be going. Katie contracted with her teacher to complete special assignments while traveling as the terms of her going. After long hugs to each of my sons at the airport, Katie and I boarded our flight from Madison to Chicago, with a connecting flight to San Francisco.

Katie started a journal, which she maintained on an almost-daily basis the whole time we were traveling. Her first entry, headlined "SPIES," was to record an unexpected overnight stay in San Francisco when our scheduled flight was delayed because of a bomb threat. All passengers were assigned rooms in a nearby hotel, and Katie was intrigued to recognize people from the plane staying in the room next to ours. Claiming that these people were spies who had followed us to the hotel, she concocted a story that they had to be carefully watched for any overt spy activities. I happily joined in her fantasy, each of us enlarging the plot with subplots before finally giving in to sleep, to be ready for the new day.

The rest of our flight, though long, was uneventful, with a brief stop in Hawaii before our arrival in Sydney. After going through Customs, we continued to Adelaide, planning to see Ian and Ros Craig on our way back to the U.S. Arriving in Adelaide, we were met by my mother, brother, and his wife Peggy, and their four children Susan, Paul, Bronwyn, and Deborah. As we pulled up in the front of Mummy's home, Katie got out of the car and promptly vomited on the front lawn! Clearly it had been a taxing journey, and the excitement perhaps a shade too much for her. However, minutes later, we were all gathered around the kitchen table, everyone but Mummy having met Katie for the first time. Katie was as fascinated with her cousins' Australian accents as they were with her strong midwestern American one. A favorite word her cousins picked up on was Katie's use of the word "guy," and soon everything was "that guy" and "this guy" in their conversations. Although her cousins were a little older than Katie, they all quickly became good mates, and were soon hanging out with her during their summer vacation from school.

December is the height of Australia's summer, so much of our time was spent on the beaches I loved so well. David's English wife, Peggy, had five sisters, all of whom were married with children, and an unmarried younger brother. So Katie's Australian family, including my sister Mary and her son, Adam, was a very large and active one, and for the next three weeks or so we enjoyed many activities in their homes and the surrounding countryside. This included observing native flora and fauna both in the wild and in reserves populated by animals such as kangaroos, koalas, and emus, much to Katie's delight. Jean, one of Peg's sisters, lived on a large property north of Adelaide, and was noted for rescuing wild animals. Some of these were baby kangaroos (joeys) whose mothers had died. On our visits to her home, we enjoyed interacting with several kangaroos that she had bottle-fed from infancy. One of these kangaroos was still bottle dependent, and when Jean visited us, she brought this joey with her in a cloth bag, which served as a substitute for its mother's pouch. She hung this bag over the back of a chair as she socialized with us, while this little fella peeked out at us from its cozy haven.

We celebrated Christmas Day at Mummy's home Australian style: a hot lamb roast with all the trimmings, followed by steam pudding and hot custard. David and I reminisced how thirty years earlier, we used to compete for multiple pudding servings, hoping to find the most silver coins Mummy had hidden in it, as was a custom borrowed from our British ancestors. Although the youngest, the skinniest, and the smallest of we three children, I had a capacious appetite and was very competitive, especially with David. As he ruefully acknowledged, I usually won this particular contest. As we continued to reminisce, David asked, "Do you remember the battle of the butter dish?" I certainly did. In those days I wasn't referred to as "Spitfire" for nothing, acknowledging that in a rage I had hurled a dish filled with butter at him. We laughingly recalled that as it landed on his nose, causing blood mingled with butter to flow over his jaw, both of us had been too shocked to continue that particular argument and quickly fled the table. Mummy had no recollection of that particular incident, but enriched the conversation with some of her own memories. Later, in the unflagging heat of the late afternoon, we all donned our swimsuits and went down to the beach to cool off with a swim. Even so, I found myself missing the snow that I had learned to love at Christmastime in America.

Katie introduced her favorite food to her new friends—peanut butter and sliced banana on white bread—and it quickly became their favorite, too. Katie's eighth birthday was less than a month away, so before we left Adelaide, the family celebrated her with a party. Her birthday gift was a record of the popular group at the time, ABBA. Katie loved it, and played ABBA constantly at every place we visited. Ever since, whenever I hear that group, my mind is filled with memories of that visit to Australia.

All too soon, it was time to leave family and friends in Adelaide. Our next destination was Melbourne to reunite with my dearest friend, Beth. In 1961, after I left the house we shared on Hackney Road to travel to the U.S., Beth traveled to England and spent two years working as a nurse in London. She had written me recounting the challenges of surviving one of England's coldest winters on record. One anecdote particularly aroused my imagination. To warm the apartment she shared with two other nurses, it was necessary to feed the primitive heater with sufficient coins to provide heat through the night. On one particularly cold night, while she slept between flannel sheets, dressed in several layers of clothes and a woolen hat pulled over her ears, the heater used up all the coins and turned off in the middle of the night. Getting up in the predawn darkness to dress for work, Beth found her white uniform, which she had washed before retiring, had slipped off its hanger and frozen like a white statue to the floor. At the time, she assured me that she looked forward to returning to South Australia's mild winters.

In October 1964, two weeks before Matt's birth, Beth had taken the long way home from England to visit Jack and me in Denver. I welcomed her loving presence at such an emotional time in my life, and after Matthew was born, she happily consented to be his godmother. Three days after his birth, she also agreed to take care of our precious little babe while Jack and I went to see the movie *Around the World in Eighty Days;* I had no hesitation in leaving him with her, my most trusted and experienced friend. I loved the temporary break from my new maternal responsibilities; however, I laughed so much at the movie that my breast milk let down, and the upper half of my pale pink dress became a very dark pink dress, much to my embarrassment! New motherhood had caught me by surprise! After Beth's too-short visit, my last image of her was of her elegantly styled long blond hair and her pencil slim skirt above her fashionably high heels as she boarded the bus to Chicago.

How sad I was to see her go, knowing how much I was going to miss her, and having no idea when I would see her again.

In 1967 Beth had joined an Australian surgical team assigned to Vietnam for a year. While there, she worked close to combat zones, caring for war casualties. Shortly before the end of her contracted year, on January 30, 1968, the hospital and medical staff were attacked by the North Vietnamese in the infamous Tet Offensive. She wrote to me that as she hid in terror under her bed, her tape machine happened to be running and had recorded the explosions, screams, and running feet all around her. On my current visit, listening to that recording of the Tet offensive was a chilling realization of how much danger she must have been in at the time.

Returning to Australia on April 10, 1968, Beth married one of the surgeons on the team, John Scott. By the time of my visit in late December 1976, they had three young children, Jo, the same age as Katie, and younger sisters, Melanie and Jenny, and were living in a large, beautiful old home in North Dandenong, a northern suburb of Melbourne. The three girls and Katie hit it off immediately, enjoying countless hours of play acting, dressing up in vintage dresses and large picture hats, and chasing each other on three wheeler bikes around the large verandah that circled the house. On January 17, the day Katie turned eight, Beth and John treated her to a second birthday party, much to Katie's delight.

In 1958 my English friend Patricia Lewis, a survivor with her family of Hitler's 1941 *Blitzkreig* bombing of London, shared a home with Beth and me in Sydney. Shortly after I left Australia in 1961, she had married a Scot, Peter McCabe; they now also had three children. Beth and Patricia invited Katie and me to join their two families on a beach vacation at Mornington Beach, south of Melbourne on Port Phillip Bay. For two days, Katie and her six playmates swam and built sandcastles on the wide sandy beaches, while I enjoyed catching up on all that had transpired with my friends since we had last been together.

Finally, it was time to set out with Katie for the last leg of our trip, to be spent with Ian and Ros in Sydney. While there, we visited the famous Taronga Park Zoo, seeing some of Australia's deadliest snakes and spiders, safely corralled behind glass. In a darkened area we also viewed some of Australia's elusive animal night life, including the rare equidna, an egg-laying mammal, the tiger quoll, the bilby, and the strange-looking duck-billed platypus. When Ian and Ros realized that Katie had just had a birthday, they surprised her by treating her to a third birthday party, her gift being a lifelike koala to remind her of Australia. What a lucky girl!

We also made several trips to Bondi, one of Sydney's most beautiful surf beaches. On our last day in Australia, as Katie boogie boarded the waves and was caught by Ian as she surged into the shore, we were having so much fun that we lost track of time. Suddenly realizing that our flight was scheduled to leave too soon for us to return to Ian and Ros' home, we made a mad dash to the airport—thankfully our bags were in the car—arriving as our names were being called as the last two passengers to board the plane. Our farewell to Ian and Ros, and to Australia, was hurried. As the plane circled over Sydney Harbor, I sought my last glimpse of the Harbor Bridge and the beautiful, recently built Opera House, wondering how long before I would see them again. Because of recrossing the international date line and regaining the day we "lost" going to Australia, we arrived in San Francisco before our departure time from Sydney. Finally, with sand from Bondi Beach still on our

Jillian, Australia, 1976.

unwashed bodies, we were greeted in Madison by Jack and the boys—and Madison's below-zero February weather.

In the months ahead, Jack and I had ongoing difficulties in negotiating the terms of our divorce, which frequently led to angry arguments. This culminated in our attorneys exchanging information with each other rather than directly with Jack or me, which was a far-from-happy solution. Finally, the court date, October 10, 1977, arrived. As Jack sat on the other side of the courtroom, with Paris at his side, Paris got up and walked over to me, with a message from Jack, "Even now, will you change your mind?" My response, "No, I cannot." My unspoken thought: "If Jack had said that months ago, perhaps my answer might have been different." My divorce settlement, more than eight years before Wisconsin passed the Shared Property law, was a harsh one. It gave little recognition to my role as wife and mother for fourteen years, including my major financial contribution in supporting Jack through four years of medical school. Although Jack was earning a high annual salary, and had significant funds in investments, my total settlement was a secondhand car, a small black-and-white television, and a small lump sum. I had no insurance coverage, no furniture, and no home. Jack was required to pay me a monthly amount of $630, which was labeled family maintenance, and taxable to me. Walking alone out to the street after our few minutes in court, I felt a deep sadness. Jack and I had made many mistakes along the way, and now we were having to live with the consequences. I had a long and unknown road ahead.

In July 1977, three months before my divorce, even as I finalized the termination of my land contract on the house in Cross Plains, I bought a four-bedroom house in Monona in time for my children to start school in the Monona School District. I still had two semesters left to earn my Master's in Behavioral Disabilities from the University of Wisconsin. My financial situation was dire, and I was frightened as to how I was going to cope. I had always been what some would call frugal—I preferred the term thrifty—in managing money. Watching my father struggle through years of financial hardship had taught me invaluable survival skills. One strategy I learned to use, especially toward the end of every month when my money often ran out, was to write all my checks in red ink, having heard that this slowed up their progress through the system. I'm not sure if that strategy actually helped, but at least I was never referred to a collection agency.

In June 1977, I completed an internship at Tellurian, a local drug rehabilitation program, as part of my Master's degree requirements. Following this, I worked in two low-paid, short-term jobs, both of which I disliked intensely,

Steve (and Benjie), Jill, Katie, (and Fifi La Foot), 1979

as I finished writing my Master's thesis. On May 28, 1978 I graduated, and when offered a salaried position by Tellurian's program director, I accepted with alacrity. Although the job sometimes required working overtime, I was familiar with the program and I enjoyed friendly relationships with the staff. I was relieved to have a job at all, with so many unknowns ahead of me as a single parent.

At 41 years old, I prepared myself for the challenges of the unfamiliar world of dating members of the opposite sex. Somewhat to my surprise, I found it was not as difficult as I imagined. One of the first relationships I had was with the brother of a friend, who introduced me to the world of long-distance running. I quickly found it not only an enjoyable activity, but I was surprised to find that I was good at it. I joined him and other runners on early morning runs and sometimes after work. I began to compete in local road races, where I won trophies on a regular basis.

By the time we were no longer dating, I was hooked on running, and it became an integral part of my life for the next twenty years or so. On many, if not most weekends, I competed in local races of varying distances, including half marathons, one marathon, and one triathlon (swimming, biking, and running.) Many races I ran on behalf of charitable causes and would ask friends and acquaintances to sponsor me for dollars per mile. Eventually I ran out of (no pun intended) sponsors and continued running just for personal enjoyment. My favorite race was the twenty-mile race from Wisconsin's State Capitol to Stoughton, a Norwegian community celebrating its former country's national day, *Syttende Mai* (May 17). I ran the hilly, challenging race five times, and was proud to do so in under three hours.

A friend gifted me with a framed poem called *Why Do I Run?* which said:

Why do I run? 'Tain't no mystery—
Wanna have a good medical history,
Doctor told me running is great—
Helps them blood cells circulate,
Great for the lungs, great for the ticker,
Can't nothin' getcha in better shape quicker,
Feels so healthy, feels so sweet,
Pumpin' my arms, and flappin' my feet,
Moldin' my muscles, firmin' my form,
Pantin' like a pack mule, sweatin' up a storm,
Keeps me youthful, keeps me loose,

Tightens my tummy, and shrinks my caboose,
Beats bein' sluggish, beats bein' lazy,
Why do I run? Maybe I'm crazy.

I ran outdoors year-round, in all weather, especially enjoying running in the winter quiet of Lake Monona under ice-laden trees sparkling like diamonds. These were my times for meditation, when my mind quieted and my problems no longer seemed so difficult.

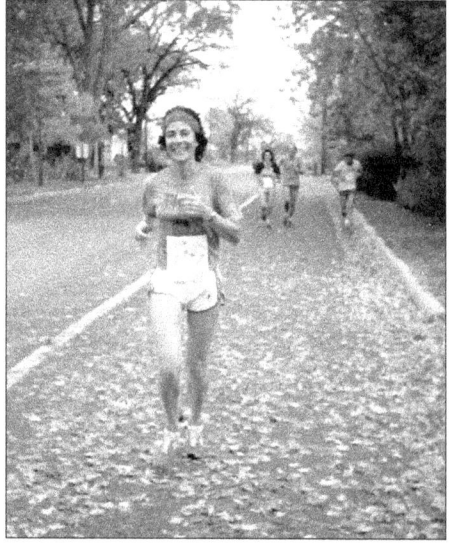

In 1979 Jack remarried, and he and his wife, Marlene, moved to New Orleans, where Jack had accepted the position of chief of transplant surgery at Ochsner Clinic. At Jack's insistence, and despite my opposition, Matt agreed to join them for his

Jill finishing Sugar River Marathon, 1980

sophomore year of school. Matt, largely left unsupervised as Jack and Marlene adjusted to their new jobs, and missing his family and friends, soon began to skip school and associate with drug and alcohol users. The situation quickly became untenable, and within a couple of months, Jack sent Matt back to live with me. For the remainder of his sophomore year, his truancy continued, but he had a bright mind and was a quick study. He passed all his courses and graduated in 1981. After graduation his behavior improved, and in 1982 he enrolled as a part-time student in real estate at Madison Area Technical College, while working as a bartender for the next two years.

Karen, whom I had first met in 1963 when we both worked in the same Denver hospital, had moved to Madison with her new husband in the early '70s, and we reconnected. Now both of us had recently ended our marriages. Karen, who was childless, became a close friend, whom my children learned to think of as Aunt Karen, and who joined us as part of our family for many activities. In early June 1978, in celebration of my graduation, Karen and I went on a ten-day trip to Jamaica, while my children stayed with Jack.

As we flew into Kingston's international airport, I remembered that my father had been stationed with the British Army in Jamaica as a newly married man some seventy years before. As I ran the Twelve Mile beach every day, I often felt his presence; were my feet walking the same pathways he had trod all those years before? One day, as I ran out to the edge of some rocks and looked into the azure sea below, I was enchanted to see many highly colored tropical fish swimming by. I recognized several as those that had been in my children's aquarium. I was glad these fish were free to swim in the sea, and I felt regret that I had thoughtlessly held the other fish captive in a glass cage those many years ago.

One day Karen and I went on a snorkeling trip to view a recently sunken boat. As I swam a few yards away from the others, I observed a large jelly fish, its tentacles appearing to reach out to me. Fascinated, I watched it as it seemed to watch me. This lasted for what seemed like several minutes—perhaps it was not really that long—when it unmistakably began to move toward me! My fascination was replaced by a jolt of fear, and I quickly backed off and joined the others, who were getting back on our expedition boat. That definitely seemed like a good idea!

On another day I rented a sailboard, something I had never tried before. I was having a great time sailing with the wind until I noticed how far away the shore had become. I began to tack the sailboard back to where I had started, but every time I tried to turn it into the wind, I fell off. This exercise in futility continued for a long time, and I was becoming exhausted. Just as I decided that I would just sail with the wind, no matter where I ended up on the shore, I heard a loud and repeated: "Coo-eee," eventually followed by "Do you need help?" I observed a person some hundred or so yards away, swimming toward me. "Yes, thank you, I do," I yelled back. A short time later, a smiling, muscled young man was hanging on to my sailboard. Instructing me to make room for him, he hauled himself on and quickly headed us toward shore. As I clung to the sides of the board, I asked him, "Are there any sharks around here?" "Could be, but I'm not worried. You're the one hanging off the end," he cheerfully responded. A Brit—with a great sense of humor!. My first vacation in several years with Karen had many new and enjoyable incidents, and the ten days away had been a lovely respite for me.

In 1981 my friend Ruth, her husband, Ed, and their three children moved to The Hague, Holland for a two-year appointment connected with Ed's work. They invited me to visit. In 1982, leaving the children with Jack, I joined them, and spent three enjoyable weeks in a world far different from my own. I continued my habit of exploring a new place by running along the many bike and horse paths abounding in Holland. On two occasions I ran all the way to the North Sea, gazing at its cold, dark waves as I imagined what it must have been like for the Dutch in German-occupied Holland of World War II. As I spoke no Dutch, I had to keep my wits about me as I ran, for if I had lost my way, I would have had no idea how to ask for directions back to Ruth and Ed's home. This, my first trip to Europe, sparked my desire and intention to return to Europe. Rather than just knowing some of my father's stories of his widely traveled family, I wanted to explore some of the places in which my ancestors had spent their lives, and sometimes their fortunes and misfortunes.

As I adjusted to the many challenges of single parenting, I would sometimes whisper to myself how grateful I was for having a strong and healthy constitution, which enabled me to work long hours, often with little sleep, to fulfill all I needed to do. Despite all we had been through over the last few years, my children seemed to be coping well with all the changes in their lives.

In 1982 I was hired by Madison General Hospital (MGH) as an RN, working as a clinician with patients having eating disorders. My financial situation greatly improved. I either rode my bike, caught the bus, or sometimes ran to and from work. Katie was doing exceptionally well as a high school sophomore, both academically and athletically. After much indecision, unlike her brothers, she decided she did not want to leave her friends at Monona High to spend a year living with Jack. This infuriated Jack, who wrote her an angry letter, accusing her of having let him down by breaking her promise to spend a year living with him and Marlene. This was deeply upsetting to Katie. Nevertheless, she remained successfully involved in her school life.

Given my healthier finances, in the summer of 1983 I decided to treat Steve and Katie, now ages 16 and 14 respectively, to a cultural experience with a trip to France, where they hopefully would improve their French. Unable to go with them, given my relatively new position at MGH, I asked Karen if she would accompany them. She readily agreed. While there, Katie called to tell me their luggage had been stolen while swimming on a French Riviera beach. She was upset at losing Bear, her favorite stuffed animal, which she had taken with her to France. She better accepted Bear's fate after we discussed that he surely would find a new home with a French child, who would love him as she did, and that he would be learning French as she was doing. Steve's only pair of glasses were in the stolen suitcase, forcing him to wear his contact lenses for the remainder of the trip. This proved difficult, as none of them knew how to ask for contact lens cleaner in French. All three of them lost most of their clothes, which required some creative thinking to

Matt, Jill, Steve, Katie, 1982

dress appropriately from then on. Nevertheless, Steve and Katie later agreed that, overall, they were glad they had gone. Karen did not complain to me on her return, but I gathered that the experience of overcoming these and other difficulties, and chaperoning and being responsible for two teenagers, had not been an entirely positive experience for her.

I was pleased with my position at MGH. Everything was going relatively well in my life, when in the summer of 1985, I received word from home that Mummy was very ill, and possibly would not survive. In response, I transferred all my scheduled patients to my colleagues, reserved a ticket to Australia, and was on the plane within 36 hours. As the plane headed west and I felt able to relax a little, I suddenly realized that I had totally forgotten to bring any money with me, and in those days, I did not have a credit card! After a moment of near panic, I realized there was nothing I could do about it, and thought, *"Que sera sera..."* Happily, I did not have a need for cash en route, and I arrived unscathed in Adelaide some 30 hours later, where I had a bank account. By then, Mummy had gone through her medical crisis, and was on the mend by the time I joined her at her hospital bedside.

Mummy's childhood best friend, who was also my godmother, Win Lamb, visited while I was there. I was able to record much of our conversation, and enjoyed hearing anecdotes from their shared lives. I also heard my mother describe how hurtful it was for her when, at the time of her mother's divorce, her three brothers had stayed with her mother, and she was sent to live with a married couple with two young daughters. She said that she was not happy or well cared for there, and that the daughters were treated much better than she was. She mentioned that for the remainder of her childhood, her mother had visited her there only occasionally, saying "she had to work, so it was difficult for her to travel from Two Wells (where she lived in the country) to North Adelaide" (where Mummy was living). This was the first time I had heard this, and perhaps explained why I had only met my grandmother once, although she lived only about forty miles from where I grew up. Each time I visited my mother at the hospital, I had a long walk down the hallway to her room. On one of these occasions, my mother commented on the sound of my high heeled shoes approaching, "You certainly have a very strong step Jilly." I sensed from my mother's words that she thought America had changed me into a more assertive woman than I had been before, perhaps for the better, perhaps not.

Toward the end of the last audiotape, David visited, and his comments were also recorded. I treasure this recording, for I did not know it at the time, but that visit was the last time I would be with my mother. She died unexpectedly on March 4, 1986, several months before my planned trip to Australia to spend that year with her. My sister Mary, suffering from terminal cancer, died eight days later, on March 12, 1986—my fiftieth birthday.

On September 27, 1985 my application to have all three of my children granted Australian citizenship was successful: they were now dual citizens of the United States and Australia. This was a rare privilege indeed, and proved to be a great advantage to all of them in the ensuing years. Even though Australia had granted citizenship to my children, the consulate refused to restore my Australian citizenship, which I had relinquished when I was granted U.S. citizenship. The Australian consul bluntly informed me, "Australians don't give up their citizenship, or if they do, they shouldn't expect to ever get it back." However, he advised me that if I was willing to follow a specific procedure of living in Australia within certain time frames, it might be possible to restore my citizenship.

Accordingly, while working at MGH, I visited Australia twice, each time for a year, from 1986 to 1987, and again from 1988 to 1989, per the procedure described to me. MGH agreed to grant me two one-year leaves of absence.

For my first trip to Australia, I applied for a one-year midwifery training program at the Queen Victoria Maternity Hospital in Adelaide. I was given a beginning date in September 1986. In preparation for my absence, I sold my house in Monona.

In 1986 Kate graduated from high school, and as I prepared to leave for a year in Australia, she started as a freshman at the University of Wisconsin, living in a campus dormitory. She was in a serious relationship with Todd Young, two years older, who would eventually become her husband; Steve was living with friends in an apartment and taking a year off from school to work at the U.S. Post Office, where he was earning a good wage; Matt was living with his girlfriend, Robin, and they were happy to have Benji, our family dog, live with them while I was gone.

It was difficult to leave them, especially with Kate just starting at the UW. Over the next year, I wrote as often as I could, and was happy to receive their letters in reply. On two occasions, they sent me an audiotape containing much laughter and joking, with stories of what they were doing, which I enjoyed. On one occasion, when I called them, I asked to talk to Benji. After a couple minutes, one of them commented, "Hey, Mom, that's enough! How about our turn to talk!" In retrospect, I came to regret that I had left my children at such a crucial time in their lives. Regaining my Australian citizenship seemed important at the time, but I came to realize it should never have taken precedence over my children's welfare. While I was gone, although none of them had any serious issues, they all missed me, and doubtless there were many times when I should have been there for them and was not.

My midwifery training was challenging, in particular because at the age of fifty, although a registered nurse, I was now a student nurse again, in an unfamiliar environment, subject to the supervision and direction of registered nurse-midwives half my age.

My first moments on my first ward proved to be an awful experience. I had just entered a room where a patient was sleeping. A young doctor rushed in and demanded that I set up an intravenous tray. Taken by surprise, my mind froze. I had no idea what to do and stood staring helplessly at him. Another nurse entered at this point and took over, while I left as fast as I could. Despite this, and other moments of difficulty, I settled into my student role and mostly enjoyed my training in a hospital completely staffed and run by midwives. My fellow trainees were also registered nurses, although all of them were much younger. They were a friendly bunch and occasionally invited me to join them at a local pub after work. On ordering a beer, one of them, Judy, bluntly informed me that "women who drink beer are considered sluts in

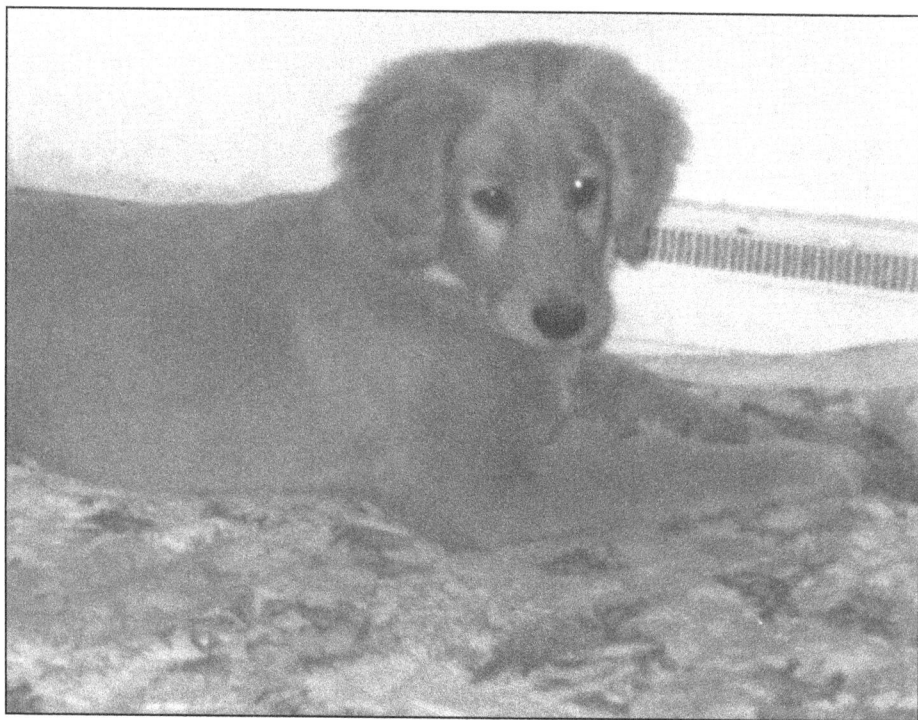

Benji, 1977

Australia." Another one, Deborah, who belonged to a religious sect unknown to me, seemed convinced that I was a sinner and did her best to convert me. When our year of training ended, as we said farewell, she expressed her hope that I would eventually be "saved." I liked this sincere young woman, but for the life of me, I had no idea why she considered me a lost soul! In September 1987 I successfully completed my training. I had passed all of my exams, and I was proud to be granted Australian certification as a nurse-midwife.

On returning to the U.S., I bought a home on Rusk Street, opposite the home of my friend Laurel Sturges. Laurel had been kind enough to keep my carpets and many pieces of furniture after I sold my home in Monona, so carrying my belongings across the street to my new home was an easy undertaking. My plan was to be home for a year before returning in October, 1988 to Australia to stay the required second year. My children were happy to have me back; Steve was starting his junior year, and Kate was beginning her sophomore year at the UW. Benji, who had spent the year I was away living with Matt and Robin, after showing his displeasure at my departure by refusing to look at me for several hours after my return, finally forgave me with a wagging tail. So all seemed to be going well with everyone. I caught up with my friends, and enjoyed getting back into my favorite activities of running, biking, and kayaking.

On returning to MGH, I was transferred from the Eating Disorders Unit to the Medical Unit. Until being hired by MGH in 1983, I had been away from the nursing profession for many years and thus I was considered the junior nurse on the unit. Every morning for the next year, I was usually assigned those needing the most basic nursing care. This was at the height of the AIDS epidemic, and there were almost always one or more AIDS patients on our unit who were invariably assigned to me. They were usually in the last stages of dying, which meant they had lost control of their bodily functions and required constant and extensive nursing care. Because they were considered highly infectious, I had to be fully gowned, masked, and gloved for several hours as I cared for these young men who were too ill to communicate with me or anyone else. This included their parents, who had been told their son was dying from pneumonia, which was only partially true. None of my patients felt able to tell their parents that their pneumonia was AIDS related and, sadly, they would die with their secret untold. It was also risky nursing. One day I accidentally stabbed myself with a possibly contaminated needle, and duly reported it. I endured many hours of worry before meeting with a social worker to learn the results of my blood test. An office visit was always required. No one was ever notified of negative results by phone because to do so would mean that requiring an office visit would indicate positive results. Needless to say, hearing the social worker report that my blood test was negative was an enormous relief!

Before leaving for my second visit to Australia in October 1988, Matt and Steve agreed to take care of Benji and to live together in my new home until my return. This was helpful for me, and I left feeling comforted knowing the brothers were together and that Benji would be well cared for.

On this visit to Australia, I worked as a psychiatric nurse in an adolescent treatment center. Although I did not have to work night shifts as I had at the Queen Victoria Hospital, I did not enjoy this position. I had become Americanized in my 27 years in the U.S., and I came to realize that I had largely forgotten how to be an Australian, at least in the world of the Australian adolescent. I had difficulty understanding their music, their social behavior, and their hostility toward adults, which not infrequently included me. However, there were occasional positive times, and, despite feeling I was not a good fit for this position, I nevertheless felt some degree of success in helping the young people in the program. I also made several friends on the staff.

Meanwhile, Kate decided to apply for her junior year at Adelaide University, having completed her sophomore year at the UW in 1988. Her application was accepted, and in November 1988 she arrived ready to start school in February 1989, the beginning of the Australian academic year. She found a lovely little house to rent, which she shared with an Australian, Jenny, and an Englishman, David, about two miles from where I was living near Brighton Beach.

I enjoyed introducing Kate to many of my friends and their young adult children, and Kate, Jenny, and David quickly became friends. After Kate's first week of school, having joined several social clubs and attended a few classes, she declared that the classes were not what she considered junior level, were uninteresting to her, and she quit. However, she took advantage of the social clubs she had joined, which offered her opportunities for an active social life. For the next several months, Kate worked parttime in two locations, as a waitress in an Adelaide Festival of Arts restaurant and as a bartender in The Earl of Aberdeen Hotel. While bartending she met many of Adelaide's socially prominent bachelors, who were attracted to this beautiful American girl and she received some interesting invitations. This included a chauffeured car to escort her to a party in the richest of the estates in the hills north of Adelaide, and a plane piloted by an admirer to fly her to another popular night spot.

Kate and I shared many good times together during the five months she was in Adelaide. I especially enjoyed her weekly Sunday pancake breakfasts, to which she invited her new friends, as well as my friends, whom she came to know and like—which I found gratifying. My most cherished memory was of the times Kate and I ran miles along the beach esplanade between our two homes, sharing the smell and the sound of the sea I loved so well. After she left Adelaide, she found work in Mt. Buller, in the eastern state of Victoria, at a ski resort. Her job was to check that all skiers had valid passes clipped to their jackets. On her first day, as she skied the upper slopes, she observed a young man with an invalid pass; she later told me that when she told him to ski down to the ski shop with her to buy the appropriate pass, she was secretly surprised—and relieved—that he did so without protest. For the entire ski season, she enjoyed not only her job, which enabled her to ski all day, but also the services of a chef who cooked all the meals for her and her fellow employees. Looking through her high glass bedroom windows to the ski slopes—her first and last view every day—she felt she had found the perfect job.

In October 1989 Kate and her friend, Richard, set out for Darwin on Australia's northern coast, across Australia's interior desert in a car without air conditioning through temperatures over 110°F. Kate described the journey "as unbelievably uncomfortable. I have never known such heat." They had no means of communication, so they were glad to find a fire station in a lonely town along the way, which had access to a radio and news of the world. The news they received was that on that very day, October 17, 1989, just as the third game of baseball's World Series was about to start in Oakland, California's Candlestick Park, adjacent to San Francisco, experienced a major earthquake. Coincidentally, I had flown into San Francisco just three days after the earthquake on my way back to Madison. It was the second biggest earthquake to ever hit the United States, and the damage and loss of life was significant.

After reaching Darwin, they stayed there for a few days in a backpacker hostel. They then felt ready to set out across the Kakadu National Park to the northeastern state of Queensland. Kate called me in the U.S. from a payphone to tell me her plans. The last words I heard were, "We'll be swimming in the caves of Kakadu, but don't worry, the crocodiles are freshwater crocodiles and don't attack like salt water crocs." As she said this, she ran out of coins, and the phone went dead. Screaming "Kate, Kate" to no avail and terrified at her totally misinformed belief, I frantically called Australia's information telephone. After the person who answered heard my story, she immediately patched me through to a backpacker hostel. A lovely young man answered. He spent the next hour or so calling every backpacker hostel in Darwin searching for Kate, in between each call assuring me he would find her. However, he never did. She was not at any of the hostels. She apparently was already on her way. I spent the next few days trying not to think of the American woman who had made Australian headlines a few months earlier. This young American woman, ignoring all the warning signs posted in the Kakadu, had gone swimming and, while others had watched, had been dragged under the water by a crocodile, never to be seen again.

About a week later, I had a cheerful call from Kate telling me she was now on the Gold Coast of Queensland, enjoying the delights of the Great Barrier Reef, the largest coral reef in the world. Although she had not been taken by a crocodile, she told me that she had actually almost lost her life while on a tour with several other backpackers. While crossing the shallow part of a river above a waterfall, she had been swept over the edge. The terrified tour guide, peering over the edge, expected to see her broken body at the base of the falls. Instead, he saw Kate clinging to a narrow rock ledge some twenty feet below, where she had managed to grab on to the protruding branches of a small bush. Someone took a picture of Kate as she was rescued with a makeshift rope, formed by jackets tied together, and hauled back onto the dry land above.

On my return to the U.S., it transpired that the rules for Australian citizenship had changed, and the government continued to refuse to grant me citizenship. So leaving my children for a total of two years, and all that that had entailed, had been for naught. (Several years later, my brother alerted me to a notice he read in his local newspaper offering an opportunity for persons to regain their citizenship. I followed up on this and was finally successful. In 1992 I joined my children in becoming a dual citizen of the U.S. and Australia.)

In November 1989, shortly after my return from Australia, I was hired as a counselor/social worker by the University of Wisconsin. For eight years, I worked as a clinician with adolescents and their families. I enjoyed this work as I felt a special affinity with troubled youth. I used my skills to help them and their families recover from the many problems they were experiencing. In 1997 I took over as Director of the program from Kathy Wolf (who was then, and has remained, a good friend) and remained in that role until my retirement in 2003.

Over those years, my children followed divergent paths.

Matt married Robin Vance in 1991, and they had two children: Reese Stephen, born May 8, 1993, and Savanna Rae, born July 24, 1997. They lived within five miles of my home, so I was able to spend time with Matt and Robin's children in their early years as their baby sitter, as well as joining both sides of the family and friends for all the family celebrations. In 1996 Matt started his own retail satellite system business, which went well through 2001. Meanwhile, he completed an associate degree in real estate, and experienced varying successes in the field of insurance, including running his own mortgage and estate development insurance business from 2001 to 2003 and founding and developing a financial service agency specializing in mortgages. Although he was uninterested in academia, he was a person of high intelligence, who frequently impressed me with his intellectual grasp of complex world affairs. He was never a joiner, rather he enjoyed individual sports and seemed fearless in whatever activity he undertook. He was an accomplished water skier and an avid scuba diver. On his many trips to snow country, he was always the one who skied from the highest snow country over the most difficult slopes, who flew over the highest jumps. Following his first experience in skydiving, he said it was the biggest high he ever had and vowed to do it again as soon as possible. This turned out to be when he jumped with his teenaged children some thirty years later! On trips with his

Matt and Jill,
Christmas, 1995

My friend
Karen, Reese,
and his mother
Robin,1993

Jill, Reese, Karen,
1993

Savanna, Matt,
and Reese, 2009

June 2011, Reese
newly graduated
from Monona
Grove High School

Savanna, 2013

*Savanna
graduated from
Monona Grove
High School,
June 7, 2015*

father, he enjoyed deep-sea fishing and relished the opportunities to partake in whatever challenge was available such as paragliding and ziplining. He recalls a helicopter tour in Maui over waterfalls, over George Harrison's estate, and over a (dormant) volcano which "looked like a moonscape." Although his natural athleticism and high intelligence were his strengths, they could also be a drawback, enabling him to grow impatient with hard and sustained efforts. This led him to move from one challenge to another, leading to "spinning his wheels" and never reaching the goals he sought.

He and Robin were divorced in 2008. At this point, Reese and Savanna were 14 and 11 years old. Happily, they were able to stay close to their father and me and they regularly spent time and overnight visits with us. Matt is a devoted father and, despite some setbacks in his life, his children have remained the main focus of his life.

In 2012 he became certified in wind and solar energy. Armed with this qualification, he traveled to Australia in hopes of getting a job in this field. He found work in an alternative energy startup company, but found many problems with the conditions and services offered. After six months, he quit and returned to the U.S. Since then, he has had varied job experiences, mostly as a sales representative for commercial insurance companies.

From the moment he entered the world, Steve exhibited an abundance of energy and interest in all things around him. He was always a loving and sensitive person, and his love of animals and nature was evident from boyhood. During his school years, he swam and played tennis competitively, and was an excellent student. In 1981, in 10th grade, he lived with Jack and Marlene in New Orleans, which proved to be a lonely and difficult year for him. He returned to Madison in June 1982 and graduated from Monona Grove High School in 1984. He graduated from the University of Wisconsin in 1990 with a BS in zoology, following which he worked in cancer research as a laboratory technician at McArdle Laboratories for one year. In 1991 he started school at the UW Veterinary School and graduated in May 1995 with a Doctorate in veterinary medicine. He worked at Elkorn veterinary clinic through 1996, then moved back to Madison, where he met his future wife. On September 8, 2002 he married fellow veterinarian, Gisela Soboll, from Dusseldorf, Germany. After their wedding, he and Gisela traveled for seven months, starting in Trinidad to visit a friend from their student veterinary days. There they thoroughly enjoyed the food, the smells, and the brightly colored clothing worn by the local people. From there they visited Tahiti on their way to spending four weeks in New Zealand, where they traveled in an

Steve visiting Ian and Ros Craig in Sydney, 2002

Steve, Gisela, Benjamin and Anja, 2011

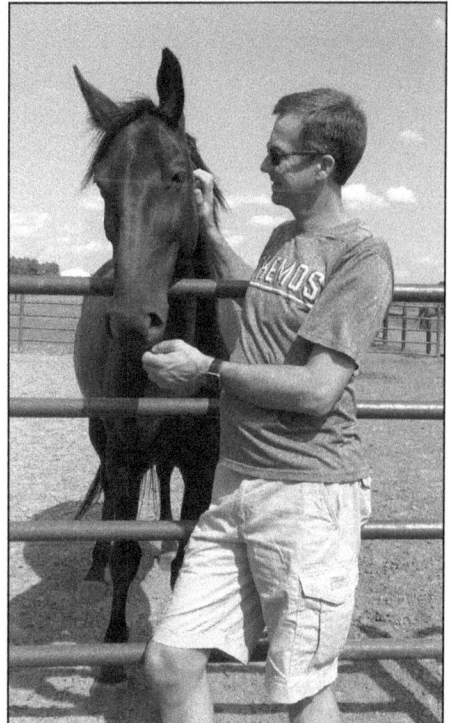

Steve the veterinarian worked mostly with horses, 2012

Steve, Jill, Anja,
Benjamin and dog
Charlie, 2012

Anja, Steve, and Benjamin, 2013

Steve's dog Charlie and cat Willow

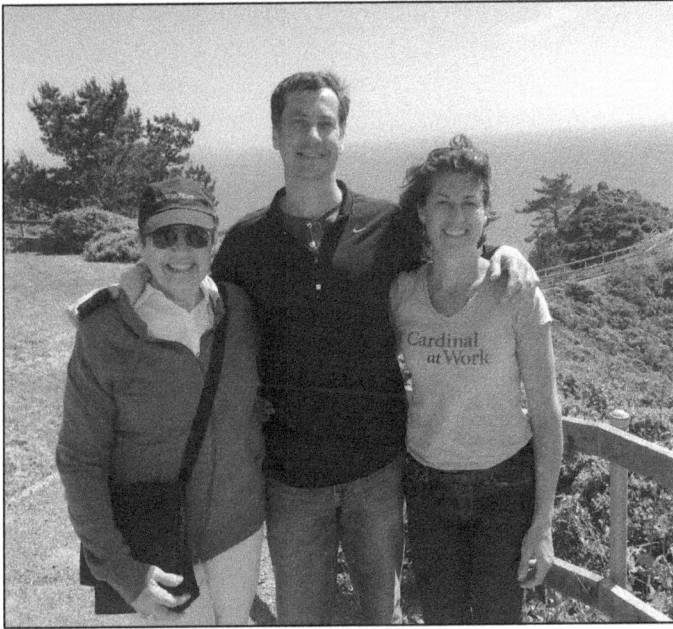

Kate, Steve, and
Jill, Muir Beach,
CA, 2017

Anja, Steve, and
Ben, July 2019, at
Todd and Kate's
home in San Jose,
California

old van they bought from some hippies. In the van, they found a cell phone, which Steve carried on a solo trip up to the top of Mt. Ngauruhoe, of *Lord of the Rings* fame, while Gisela waited below. In the U.S., I received an excited call from him as he looked down into the volcano, warning me: "The view is amazing, but I only have about two minutes on this phone before it dies," which it did right after those words. They hiked in forests, rappelled down cliffs into caves, and swam and scuba dived before heading to Australia.

In Australia, Steve and Gisela visited the beautiful but very different cities of Sydney and Melbourne, after which they spent three weeks hiking in the cold and rugged country of Tasmania, where they reported seeing lots of snakes. Finally, they rented a van and drove to Adelaide and met Steve's Uncle David and Auntie Peg, and their many cousins, and swam off the local beaches of Seacliff and Brighton. They then traveled through Australia's desert interior, through Coober Pedy, where 95% of the world's opals are found, and where the people live underground because of temperatures that often exceed 115°F, up to Darwin on the northern coast. They found this city "very unsettling, like it was about to explode," because of tensions between the whites and the Aborigines, and where they often observed drunken fighting between the local people. The last city they visited was Brisbane, capital of the eastern state of Queensland, where they stayed with Ian and Ros Craig's son, Jon, before heading on to Southeast Asia.

They flew into Bangkok, Thailand, and found they loved the culture, the high energy, and the good food. In Nepal they trekked in the mountains. On one occasion they were caught in a blizzard. Although they were accompanied by a guide, as they passed gravestones of people who had not made it, they felt afraid and were glad to make it back to level ground. They also visited Cambodia, Laos, and Vietnam, countries that had been devastated in what the citizens call the "American War." They rode on elephants, visited temples and museums, as well as the tunnels built by the Vietcong during the war. They were surprised to find that the people "liked us as Americans." They flew out of Bangkok to Düsseldorf for a week's visit to Gisela's parents before flying back to Madison in March 2003.

Steve and Gisela moved to New Hampshire In December 2003, where their first child, Benjamin Bourne Hussey, was born on June 20, 2004. In October 2005 they moved to Colorado, where Anja Isabella was born on March 18, 2006. In July 2012 they moved to Michigan, where they currently live. Sadly, Steve and Gisela gradually grew apart, and in 2014 they were divorced. However, they have maintained an amicable relationship, and to this day I have been able to continue to stay involved in Benjamin's and Anja's lives.

Kate graduated from the UW in May 1992, with a degree in psychology. She married her sweetheart from Monona Grove High School, Todd Young, on September 6, 1992 and they then moved to Chicago. In May 1996 she graduated with a Master's degree in psychology from Loyola University. On February 27, 1997 their first child, Alexander John, was born. In May of that year they traveled with Alex to Germany for four weeks, following which they returned to live in Madison in June 1997. Erik Edward was born on September 29, 1999, and Rebecca Katherine on January 17, 2002.

Other than the four years that Todd and Kate lived in Chicago while they were in graduate school, they lived in Madison, and I was able to enjoy a close relationship with them and with their three children. Much of my time with the family revolved around attending many sports activities, including basketball, baseball, football, soccer, tennis, and other athletics, as well as waterskiing, at which all five of them are accomplished. So when Todd's job ended at Oscar Mayer in 2016 and he was forced to relocate, it was a difficult adjustment for us all. I missed my daughter and her family very much.

From 2008 to 2016 Kate worked at the UW in neuropsychology in childhood epilepsy research. In 2016 when the family moved to San Jose, California, where Todd accepted a position at Apple, Kate became the coordinator of a research program in osteoarthritis of the knee in the radiology department at Stanford University. Since then, I have made many visits to San Jose, and they have returned to Madison for special occasions such as birthdays, Thanksgiving, and Christmas. So life moves on, Kate and Todd and the children are happy in their new jobs, schools, and environment. I can now look forward to my visits to the wonderful climate and energy of California, which, for many reasons, reminds me of the climate and way of life I enjoyed growing up in Australia.

Todd, Erik, Alex, Rebecca, and Kate, 2008

07/12/2008

Kate and Todd's daughter Rebecca and Jill's dog Sally, 2010

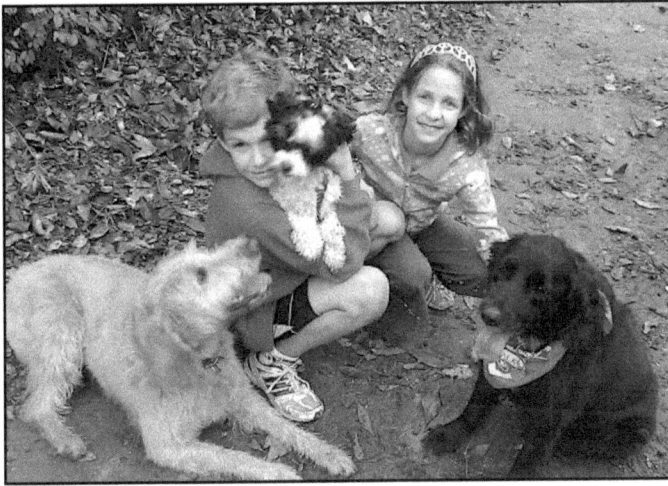

Erik and Rebecca, with dogs Sally, Coco and Susie, 2012

Kate and Todd's son Erik playing guitar, 2010

Todd and Kate, Rebecca, Alex, and Erik and dog Coco, 2016

Rebecca, Kate, Alex, and Erik,
Mother's Day Run, 2017

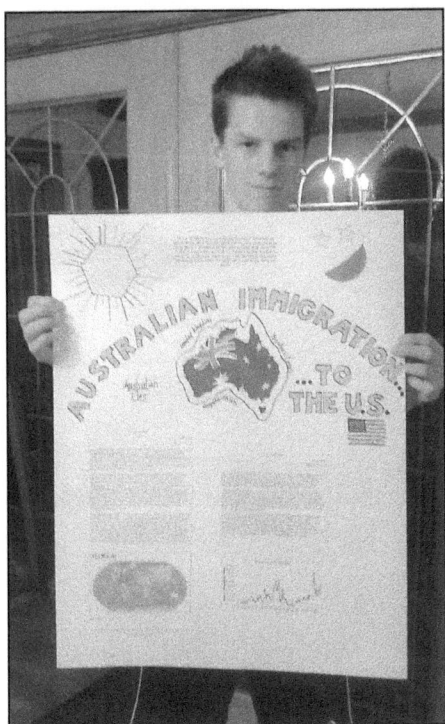

Kate and Todd's
son Alex writes of
his grandmother's
immigration, 2012

Jillian, newly divorced, summer 1979

Chapter 6

The abiding interests and activities of my life have been my love of animals, helping to preserve the environment in which we all live, and working for political and social justice. I was blessed with good health and a love of travel, which, combined with an unquenchable curiosity, guided my choices and decisions in following these interests. My love of animals, both domestic and wild, is threefold: to be in their company whenever possible, to commit to protecting them, and to outlaw their exploitation in whatever way I am able. My political activism was extensive in the human realm, but not infrequently was also necessary on behalf of animals.

My earliest memories are of the sea, and wherever I may be living, it beckons me: Come back! Whether putting on my running shoes while visiting The Hague and running to the North Sea or whale watching on a clipper ship, the *Harvey Gamage,* in the Stellwagen Sanctuary on the Atlantic Ocean or driving around the Great Australian Bight with my friend Pam Thomas and her sister, Maggie, to Aborigine-owned land at Yalata, where, with Aboriginal permission, we watched from the cliffs as the southern right whales and their calves surfed the Southern Ocean waves on their five-month visit from winter in Antarctica, I am spiritually nourished when I am reunited with the sea.

As a child, I used to dream of owning a place for all the hungry, discarded, and suffering animals in the world, where I could look after them until I could find homes for them. This dream never eventuated, but as an adult I have been an activist on behalf of animals, both domestic and in the wild. In order to write letters, to attend and speak at legislative hearings, to meet with legislators and other policy and decision makers, and to achieve any degree of effectiveness, I had to speak from knowledge. I had to learn the harsh realities of animal suffering, whether it be in research laboratories,

puppy mills, slaughterhouses, factory farms, circuses, rodeos, or other
forms of abuse. I have worked with
many like-minded people over the
years. We have supported each other,
shared the pain of not being able to
do enough, and rejoiced in whatever
victories, no matter how small, that
we have achieved.

Life and death have always held
me in their grasp. No older than eight
or nine, I recall the thrill of watching
a foal being born and marveling at
its ability to rise on shaky legs from
the ground immediately after its
birth and follow its mother around

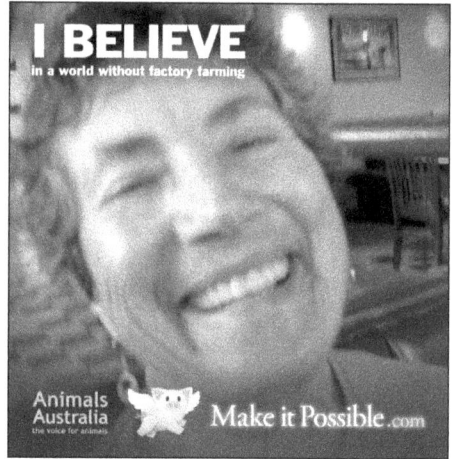

*I Believe in a World Without
Factory Farming*

the paddock. From the wonder of watching our cats and dogs give birth as
I grew up, to the miracle of childbirth as a nurse-midwife, I have never lost
this love of and respect for all life.

One of my happiest memories of animal protection work is the four
summers I spent on Folly Island, South Carolina. There I joined my friend,
Broxanne Spencer, a formal member of Loggerhead Turtle Watch, which pro-
tects the turtles that come to the beach to lay their 100 or so eggs. Whenever
heavy turtle tracks were found coming from the sea up into the sand hills,
one of the members would respond by locating and roping off the nest, noting the relevant date of eggs laid, and the estimated hatching date. As an
informal member of the Turtle Watch, I patrolled the beach with Broxanne
every morning and evening, as well as once at night, to be sure that the
many nests along the beach had not been invaded, either by humans or by
animals, including the dreaded red ants.

Our night visit was to ensure that there were no outdoor lights from
nearby homes visible from the beach. This was necessary, for when the turtles hatched they instinctively headed for the sea. However, a light could
confuse them and steer them away from the sea and toward certain death.
Many were the times that I was present when the turtles hatched. To see these
tiny creatures clamber out of the deep nest and watch their tiny legs rapidly
carry them to the shore, plunge into the sea, lift their heads for a quick look
around, then dive back under the waves and head for the ocean depths is an
incredible, heartwarming sight. A sad thought, however, was knowing that

because of the many dangers of the sea, only about one of the hundred or so would live to adulthood, and eventually return to lay her eggs on this same beach many years later.

In September 1996 I was a participant on a whale and dolphin identification expedition on Monterey Bay, California, a National Marine Sanctuary, aboard a 55-foot motor vessel, the *Point Sur Clipper*. For seven days we had frequent encounters with humpback whales, once sighting a one-hundred-foot-long blue whale, the largest animal to have ever lived on earth. I observed a rich variety of marine life, including seals, sea lions, and otters, many varieties of birds, and frequent pods of more than 1,000 dolphins.

Whenever we became aware of whales in our vicinity, the captain would stop our boat for the scientists to photograph and identify the whales. The whales were clearly aware of our presence and would sometimes entertain us by "spy-hopping" (lifting up their heads to look around), "lobtailing" (slapping their tails), and breaching. They would frequently swim around and under our boat. On one occasion as I stood on the gunwale (side) of our boat, I looked directly down and became aware of a whale's enormous eye just below the surface, looking directly into my eyes. Our eyes held for a long moment, then the whale began to slowly rise from the water, its huge body within inches of mine as she rose, higher and higher. As I stood there, mesmerized, I could have touched her gleaming body, but did not do so. I felt an intense connection with her as she remained suspended in front of me then slowly lowered back into the sea, and disappeared under the boat. Moments such as this have remained unforgettable and vivid memories with me.

Following the whales on both sides of the world included a camping trip in February 1996 on a desert island in Baja, Mexico with sixteen women, and kayaking every day with the California Gray whales in Laguna San Ignacio. We started out as strangers, women from all walks of life, but by the end of our adventure, we had shared many wonderful experiences and formed close and caring friendships. We all first met in Los Angeles as we prepared to join a flight to La Paz, Mexico.

In La Paz our group stayed overnight at the Hotel Lorimar, a small hotel with open windows—and no screens or bugs—which was seemingly dominated by a colorful Macaw with a great personality. This parrot followed us about, turning up everywhere, even in our rooms as we readied to retire at night.

Before dinner we met in the courtyard with our expedition leaders, Ann Linnea and Christine Baldwin. I had met Ann, author of *Deep Water Passage…A Spiritual Journey at Midlife* some months before at one of her book readings. As an experienced kayaker, I was drawn by her account of her solo, and often perilous, journey circumnavigating Lake Superior, the first woman to do so in a kayak. In conversation with her, she invited me to be part of the women's group she and Christine were forming to kayak with the Gray whales, to which I readily agreed.

While we drank delicious margaritas, Christine, author of *Calling the Circle*, had us form our first "circle," which was to be an integral part of our experience for the next week. She described the circle "as a form of social intimacy, each of us choosing to tell her story, and each of us retaining responsibility for our own privacy issues." At the end of circle, Christine encouraged us to spend a few minutes writing down our thoughts.

This is what I wrote:

Once there was a woman who awoke on a day of sun
She felt the life-giving warmth permeating her body
Felt the peaceful light on her face.
With the sun the ice melts the northern polar caps
and the Southern Antarctic.
Hope is renewed where all had seemed dark and lonely
New ideas were born where there seemed a dearth of possibilities
From a time of ignorance, of hurt too deep to acknowledge
Came the tiniest buds of hope, of renewal
Of giving up hate and loathing for others
And most of all the self
Of realizing that a new day had begun
And every day hence could be a day of new light
New learning, new awareness
Some days more than others
And on days where little or nothing seemed to have changed
There was the memory of the sun
And rebirth, renewal, regeneration.
Could there be life elsewhere?
Could the beauty of the world as we know it
Be somewhere another world similar to ours
Perhaps thousands of times over?
Where there is sun there is light, there is life, there is hope for a better world
Either this one or one we have yet to know.

After piling our luggage and camping equipment on the roof of our bus, we crossed the mountains and desert from La Paz to Puerto Lopez Mateos on Baja, Mexico's Pacific coast. As we unpacked our belongings onto a twenty-five-foot-long wooden *panga* (motor boat), we were excited to be on our way to a small island in Magdalena Bay, where we would be the only inhabitants for seven days of kayaking with the fifty-foot-long California Gray whales and their newborn calves. Juan, our panga driver, was a fisherman for most of the year, but in the whaling season he was licensed to deliver people and goods to the islands of Magdalena Bay, thus enhancing his family income. He was a warm and friendly man, and we enjoyed getting to know him over the next week.

Our small island was one of many. On our first full day, leaving in the early morning, we kayaked north along channels through the lagoons and under the overhanging mangroves to some nearby islands. Wherever we were, we were always surrounded by thousands of birds: osprey, blue herons, seagulls, geese, ducks, and brown and white pelicans. The pelicans were spectacular as they flew fast and low in formation, then diving into the water to catch a fish. The birds showed no fear of us and would allow us to kayak, or when we pulled over, to walk close to them. It was quiet and peaceful, and especially beautiful in the morning and early evening light. On the way back to camp that first day, we ventured into the main channel, coming close to the mouth of the Pacific Ocean. A group of whales appeared and surrounded us with their calves. Some of the mothers came within five or six feet of us, nudging their babies toward us, as if showing them off. On our way back to camp, some of them followed us for quite a long distance before disappearing into the sea.

We had many such encounters with the whales; they seemed as interested in us as we were in them. Many times they stayed near our kayaks. Encouraged by their mothers, the calves would glide up to a kayak, their baby two-ton-bodies slowly rising out of the water as they spy-hopped, opened a huge eye, and took a long look at one of us. I can think of nothing more captivating than to be so observed!

On one occasion, for about twenty minutes, we watched them feeding, as they rolled over, showing their flukes and tails, and as they rolled back, allowing us to see their eyes and blow holes. On another occasion, we saw several males mating with a female, a never-to-be forgotten sight! We were often treated to the spectacular sight of these fifty-foot-long, thirty-ton Grays breaching two, three consecutive times, their enormous bodies lifting completely out of the water, then crashing back into the sea, sometimes only a few hundred yards from our kayaks. We felt no fear. Rather, we shouted with joy at the sight. I would find myself close to tears, longing to join them in the mysterious depths below. Magdalena Bay is one of the main calving and mating areas for the California Grays. I found it hard to reconcile their trust and interest in us, knowing that they had been mercilessly slaughtered to the point of near extinction in the nineteenth, and again in the early twentieth centuries, as they ferociously tried to protect their calves in these very waters, only to reappear in the tens of thousands in the 1960s. Considering that whales can live up to 100 years, some may still live with these memories. Indeed, there are reports of some Grays being seen who still bear harpoon scars. They are now protected by the Mexican government. Perhaps the whales know this.

One day we went by panga to Magdalena Island, which is covered with miles of incredibly beautiful sculpted sand dunes, uninterrupted by any animal or human footprints. It also has a spectacular beach, covered with thousands of sea shells. We went for a brief swim, and as we languished in the warmth of the sand dunes, we saw a whale spy-hopping close to the shore, watching us, doubtless finding a large group of human females lying in the sun an unusual and interesting sight!

Every morning and evening, and sometimes in between, a pod of dolphins would come down the channel to within a few feet of our camp, as they cruised and danced on their way to the inner lagoons. One early morning while I was swimming alone, a pod unexpectedly appeared and stayed near me for a few magical moments, making mid-air leaps, flips, and somersaults before continuing on their way. Fifty years before, as a child swimming by myself in the shallows of the sea near my home, I had a similar experience. A small group of dolphins suddenly appeared and delighted me as they briefly danced and leaped in the water around me, and then left, all too soon.

All our meals were outstanding. Each of us took turns assisting our cook, Alexis, a biologist and ecologist in her "other life"; her daily breakfasts of oatmeal, pancakes, scrambled eggs, and fruit were the best I've ever enjoyed. Alexis seemed an old soul, wise beyond her years, knowledgeable about nature, her ambition being to educate as much as possible people of the world, children especially, on environmental issues. Given her knowledge, combined with her gentle nature and grace, I felt sure she would be successful in her ambition.

After every dinner we formed in circle and shared our stories. We listened, laughed, and cried with each other, and learned from each other. In the center of our circle, on a protected island where fire was forbidden, we created a sacred altar of seashells and treasures found in the sand, as we listened to the sounds from the sea and gazed at the stars in the inky black sky. We followed circle with dancing, singing, drawing in the sand, and chanting to the beat of Alex's drum, igniting our pagan souls!

Every morning we awoke to the sounds of the sea, to the breathing of the whales, sometimes to the cries of the coyotes. They were also the last sounds we heard as we fell asleep. At dawn on our last morning, coyotes on a nearby island, where we had frequently seen adult and pup coyote footprints in the sand, filled the air with a wild chorus of voices as we prepared to leave this spiritual place and the gentle giants of the deep who had shared their lives with us over the past week. It was with great sadness that I looked back at the island as our panga headed to Puerto Lopez Mateos—back to my every-day life!

In my fifty years or so of working on behalf of animals, talking with legislators, attending and speaking in support of animal protection bills at legislative hearings, writing letters and taking every opportunity to speak publicly on behalf of animals, I have had to struggle to maintain my optimism in the face of heart-wrenching setbacks. The prejudicial slaughtering of wolves, the violence of bear baiting, dog and cock fighting, pig wrestling, the breeding of nonhuman primates for lives of isolation in small metal cages for research experimentation, where many of the animals literally go mad from the conditions and torture they endure, have fueled my efforts to work with like-minded activists to be a voice for animal rights. So many examples of cruelty and suffering, and yet there also have been heartening examples of increased public awareness and support for new policies and efforts to protect animals. Although there are many battles ahead, every victory, no matter how small, is reason to celebrate and to maintain the effort on behalf of defenseless animals.

When my children were growing up, one of our favorite weekly shows was Jacques Cousteau's sea explorations, sharing his love of sea creatures and his passion for preserving their environment. Sometimes they would tease me about my admiration of his life, suggesting that if I could, I would give up my life as their mother and join him in his adventures. Of course they knew that wasn't possible, but perhaps they were correct that my fantasy was to live as he did— close to the sea—and to influence others to care about its creatures and the health of the oceans. My children have developed into sensitive human beings, who love and cherish animals as I do, and who follow the edict to "tread lightly on the earth."

Although in my early years I was not politically active, I recall many heated discussions with my Australian friends about the lack of rights for indigenous Aborigines, who were denied the right to be citizens of their native land. These discussions led nowhere, but instilled in me a sense of the many injustices toward those different from the mainstream, and the underlying and frequently overt, racial prejudice. I was taught little about the history of the indigenous people who had lived on this island continent for at least 40,000 years before the arrival of the Europeans. Through murder, disease, and marginal living conditions, their numbers were reduced from the original 1 million to the current population of about 60,000. Aborigines were not given citizen status until 1967, and were pushed to either mission settlements in remote and barren areas of the country or to city fringes.

Some Aborigines were given the opportunity to work for pay on sheep and cattle stations, where they proved to be skilled horsemen and good workers, at least until they would suddenly decide to "go walkabout" and disappear for months at a time. Many were the discussions I had with friends who employed these men, defending them against assertions that they were hopeless and untrustworthy because of this tendency to disappear. Clearly they were different from us and had difficulty adjusting to our ways, but that didn't make them stupid and ignorant as claimed. In fact, they were sometimes employed by police to track escaping criminals across the outback, and because they could "read" the land in a way that no European could, they invariably were able to find the fugitive.

In 1968, with the passage of the Aboriginal Land Rights Act, they slowly began to regain some of the land forcibly taken from them since the coming of Europeans. The common attitude toward them has been that they are dirty and undesirable, and that they have the limited mental capacity of an uncivilized people from the Stone Age. Slowly, as they begin to gain a foothold in the dominant society, this attitude is changing. When I occasionally saw the squalor of their living situations, or observed them in public places, I felt sad for a people so degraded and living in such hopeless poverty. Even so, as a child, I knew that they had been a unique people before their culture had been largely destroyed. Until my mother got wind of it, I demonstrated my admiration for their past by telling my classmates that I was part Aborigine. My mother demonstrated her Australian upbringing by squelching that fantasy in no uncertain manner!

Every day on my way home from school in Adelaide, South Australia's capital city, I bought the daily newspaper, *The News,* and avidly read all the political news on the forty-minute train ride home. I would look out the train's window as it passed the ugly gray walls of the Adelaide Jail. I would consider how miserable the lives of the men behind those stone walls had to be. I had heard stories of Aborigines being imprisoned there who died there. These deaths would be rationalized by people as the difficulty Aborigines experienced being corralled behind walls, but I felt much more likely their deaths were the result of the maltreatment they endured when behind those walls.

In 1954 I no longer traveled home on the train every day. As a student nurse, my new home was the Nurses' Home in North Adelaide. Four years after graduating as a registered nurse, from 1961 to 1963, sponsored by the American Nurses Association, I worked as a nurse in the U.S. In 1964 I married Jack Hussey, a decision that changed the direction of my life. Having made the decision to live in the United States instead of returning to Australia as I had intended, I was forced to relinquish my Australian citizenship when I became a U.S. citizen in 1972.

As the war in Vietnam escalated under the presidency of Lyndon Johnson, by which time I was the mother of three small children, I felt compelled to get involved against it. My actions became increasingly involved with other activists, and while Richard Nixon was president, we became aware that our phones were being tapped and that we were probably on what was known as his Enemies List. Although this did not deter me, I was nevertheless worried that as a new citizen I may have been taking a risk by attracting the government's negative attention. For some time I had been withholding a portion of my taxes in protest against the war, but after receiving a letter from authorities warning me that I could go to jail for this, I backed down and reluctantly began paying in full. My sister-in-law, Kathleen, who was married to a U.S. Marine fighting in Vietnam, was angry at my antiwar activities. This caused a rift between us, as it did in many families who held opposite views of the rightness of the war. The war eventually ended, but Kathleen's negative feelings toward me did not.

In 1972 I returned to school and in January 1975 I was granted my B.S. in Psychology, and in May 1978 my M.S. in Rehabilitation Counseling and Psychology. My political activism continued, with much of my energy focused on disparities of the legal system in which I saw two levels of "justice"; those—mostly white—with money and influence, versus people of color, who with every passing decade, increasingly filled the jails and prisons disproportionate to their population and level of crime. As a social worker and counselor, I saw these disparities borne out in people of color, people caught up in systematic cycles of poverty, and the lack of resources available to them once caught up in the legal system.

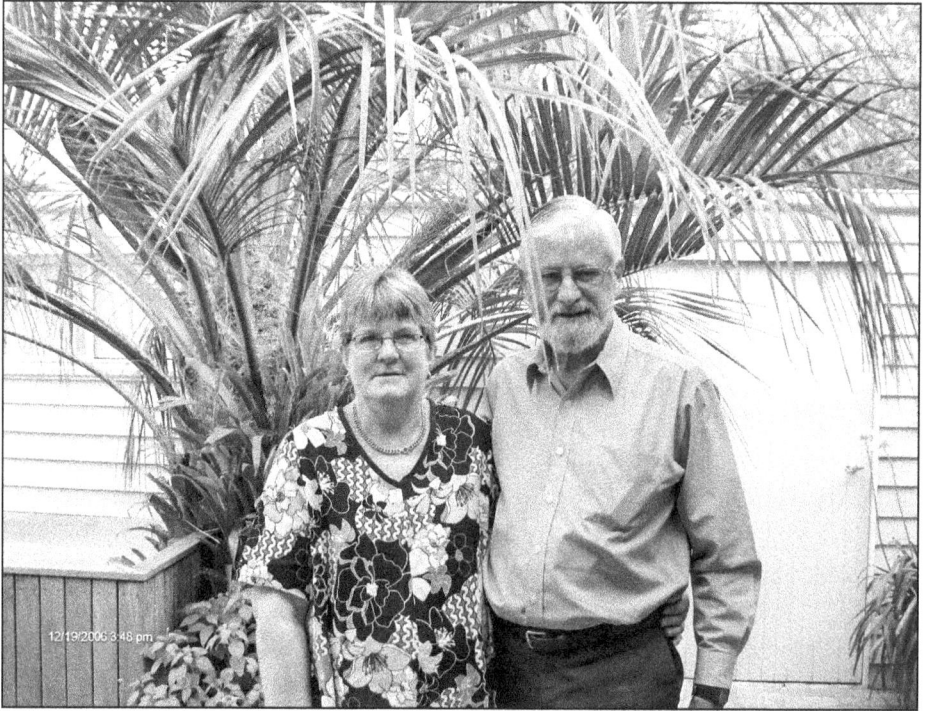

Beth and John Scott, December, 2006

Some of my ongoing activities over the years included bearing witness at the School of the Americas, Ft. Benning, Georgia, against the atrocities committed by dictators trained at Ft. Benning against people from Central American countries; the Million Mothers March Against Guns in Washington, D.C., Occupying D.C. in Washington, D.C., and protest marches against the mining industries jeopardizing and destroying environmentally sensitive areas; protest marches against the 1991 Gulf War.

In October,1992, I joined the First International Minoan Celebration of Partnership. Greece's First Lady, Margarita Papandreou, welcomed us to Crete, saying: "On this very soil, Crete, where the Minoan civilization flourished in peace for thousands of years." Activists from all over the world were there to work together to create new models to help solve societal problems. The seven day celebration offered us new ways of thinking to restructure a cooperative society of equality for men, women and children, economic equity, harmony with nature and conflict resolution without violence. Most of us were inspired, but we also understood that this was a challenge which would require hard work and determination for generations to come if we were to achieve a more humane, less dominant society.

Young Ziggy in snow, 2011

In 2008 I worked many hours knocking on doors, making phone calls, and attending meetings on behalf of presidential candidate Barack Obama. On November 6, I was in a predominantly black district in Milwaukee as a poll watcher on election day. What a day! We were overjoyed to see him elected as the first black president of the United States. Again, in 2012, after once again working hard on his behalf, it was equally exciting to see him re-elected for a second term.

I have taken my responsibilities seriously as a citizen of this great country. By my words and examples, I have encouraged my children to do the same. I am proud of all three of them, as I observe that they, in turn, encourage their children to be hardworking, peace-loving, responsible citizens.

I quote Kahlil Gibran, whose words I have tried to keep in mind as I raised my children:

Your children are not your children,
They are the sons and daughters of Life's longing for itself.
They come through you but not from you,
And though they are with you yet they belong not to you.

You may give them your love but not your thoughts,
For they have their own thoughts,
You may house their bodies but not their souls,
For their souls dwell in the house of tomorrow, which you cannot visit,
Not even in your dreams.

Ziggy and me, 2019

Acknowledgments

My many thanks to author and editor Sarah White for her invaluable suggestions and encouragement in the writing of this book. In our monthly meetings over the past eighteen months, she acted as my sounding board as I explored my memory. There were times when I gratefully accepted her judgment as to what could be included in my story, and what could be left out. I valued her advice and guidance, her insights and her literary astuteness, without which writing this book would have been much more difficult for me to accomplish.

I am indebted and deeply grateful to Robert Griffiths, my father's grandson, and my nephew and friend, for his invaluable knowledge of our family history, and for his up-to-date Griffiths Family Tree, all the way to the latest addition of my cousin, Patricia Robitaillie's third great grandchild, Octave—the first male child born since Patricia's father Noel Griffiths in 1896.

Robert demonstrated amazing patience in answering my countless questions, sometimes more than once, as I struggled to succinctly describe the complexities of our shared ancestry. Over the years, Robert has sent me many pages of research that he has compiled about the different branches of our family. These writings I plan to organize into one volume in the very near future, so that any interested descendants can learn more about their ancestors.

For now, those who would like to learn more can visit http://thepeerage.com/p23241.htm#i232406.

Epilogue

Griffiths Family History

There were some colorful characters amongst my ancestors, and I will briefly recount two anecdotes to give you a sense of what I mean. In order to identify the complexities of my ancestors' relationships, I have included two partial segments of my Family Tree. Please be aware that the dates in the Family Tree are noted using the British system of recording the day first, followed by the month and year.

I am also including a one-page background history, compiled by my nephew, Robert Griffiths, of **Sir Robert Offley Ashburton Crewe-Milnes,** the first and last Marquess of Crewe. I have done this given the possibility that some of my descendants may be interested in understanding his biological relationship to my grandfather, **Rev. Talbot Monckton Milnes Griffiths.**

My great grandfather, **John Griffiths,** was born on the September 15, 1813, in Byford, Herefordshire, the illegitimate son of the 2nd Baron Crewe, known as the "Bad Baron." Discreet arrangements were made with a local childless couple, John and Ann Griffiths, to claim that this child, named John, (later to become the Rev. John Griffiths), was their biological son. At the time, John Senior was aged 47, and Ann was aged 46, her age adding credence to the belief that she had not actually given birth to John.

Besides John, the Baron had fathered an illegitimate daughter by an unknown woman whom he "married" in the chapel of Crewe Hall. This was a bogus marriage, conducted by the Baron's billiard marker, dressed as a parson. As a result of this union, a daughter was born. Both John Griffiths and this daughter were acknowledged by the Baron's legitimate daughter, the Hon. Annabella Hungerford Crewe, as her half siblings. When the Baron's scandalous behavior became known, he was banished from England, living the remainder of his life in Liege, Belgium, forbidden to ever return to England.

Annabella Crewe subsequently married Richard Monckton Milnes, the 1st Baron Houghton of Houghton, in the West Riding of Yorkshire. Their son, Robert Offley Ashburton Milnes, was born on 12 January, 1858. Robert's cousin, my grandfather, Talbot Monckton Milnes Griffiths, son of John Griffiths, was born on June 11, 1855. (The names Houghton, Monckton and/ or Milnes continued to be included in the names of many subsequent Griffiths male descendants, through to Paul David Milnes Griffiths, my brother David's son.) Although their lives would follow different paths, Robert Milnes' and John Griffiths' relationship as cousins was well known and acknowledged by both family and local villagers alike.

Talbot Monckton Milnes, son of the Rev. John Griffiths and Frances Mortlock, was born on November 6, 1855 in Waltair, India. He was educated at Ipswich School, London and Keble, Oxford. In 1884, he married Mabel Ida Anderson, who was born in Mangalore, India on January 4, 1861. For many years he served as an army chaplain in the British Army in India, where he was recognized as one of India's first-class shots. This was borne out by his many shooting prizes won at Bisley, the top rifle shooting venue and Headquarters of the National Rifle Association in the United Kingdom. On retiring from the army in 1901, he had accepted a 'living' at the Anglican Church in Warmingham, Cheshire, where my father and his five younger siblings spent their remaining adolescent years. Based on a letter in Grandfather's handwriting, it was evident that this position was acquired with the help of Grandfather's cousin, Robert Milnes, at that time the Earl of Crewe. Talbot Monckton Milnes served as the rector at the Anglican Church in Warmingham, Crewe until his death in 1929.

Robert Offley Ashburton Milnes was educated at Harrow School, London, and Trinity College, Cambridge University, Cambridge, graduating with an M.A. in 1885. He succeeded as the second Baron Houghton shortly thereafter. He had his last name legally changed to Crewe-Milnes on June 8, 1894 and on July 17, 1895 he became the first Earl of Crewe. He was created first Marquess of Crewe on June 22, 1911. Following a distinguished political career, including Lord-Lieutenant of Ireland, Secretary of State for India, Ambassador to France, and Secretary of State of War in 1931, he died childless on June 20, 1945, making him the first and last Marquess of Crewe.

Following the birth of Talbot and Mabel's first child, **Theodore Ralph Houghton Griffiths**, in Cuttack, India, on August 10, 1886, Robert Milnes, having just succeeded as the second Baron Crewe, accepted the request to become Theodore's godfather. There are many indications that Theodore, my father, always known by his third given name, Houghton, enjoyed an amicable relationship with his godfather. This included occasionally playing chess with Lord Crewe, and being invited to attend some of the social functions at Crewe Hall. Family lore includes the story that at one of these functions, when Houghton was a junior officer in the British Army, at the request of another British Army officer—Winston Churchill—he introduced Churchill to his future wife, Clementine Ogilvy Spencer.

Houghton had grown up always knowing that he would be a soldier, coming from a long line of male ancestors who were either soldiers, seamen, or Church of England ministers. He spent the first seven years of his life in India. Then, as was traditional in those days, he was sent to England for schooling. In 1893 he entered Denstone School, Uttoxeter, Staffordshire where he was eventually in the shooting VIII and became a School Prefect in 1902. In November, 1904 he received a commission in the North Staffordshire regiment as Second Lieutenant in the British Army. He writes of his father's disappointment when he refused to follow in Talbot's footsteps and become a minister in the Church of England. He also declined the offer of Lord Crewe to take over the management of the Crewe Estate, so determined was he to become a soldier. As his daughter, I have speculated how the family history would have changed if he had accepted that offer.

In 1992 I visited Talbot's church. I was fortunate to meet the local bell-ringers, who invited me to join them in the belfry at their weekly practice. I readily agreed to do so.

As we walked through the church and into the antechamber behind the altar, I observed a picture on the wall of Grandfather. As we continued up the winding stairs to the belfry, I was aware of my feet treading the same steps that my grandfather must have trodden so many years before. I was strongly aware of my grandfather's presence, and felt that he was welcoming me! After my new friends finished their practice, I happily accepted the offer of one of them to visit his 92-year-old father-in-law, who had been one of my Grandfather's choir boys in the 1920s. What followed was a fascinating hour or more of listening to, and recording, this sparkling-eyed, uninhibited storyteller offering me anecdotal memories of my biological family from eighty years before. This gifted raconteur also commented on Talbot being "in with the upper class" by being "Lord Crewe's cousin." I was impressed with the old man's matter-of-fact reference to the cousinship, his words affirming for me that Lord Crewe's and Grandfather's relationship was common knowledge in the village.

As noted earlier, the Rev. John Griffiths married Frances Mortlock, 29 years old, on January 25, 1844. They moved to Madras, India, where he served as Senior Chaplain in the Church of England. Frances Mortlock was the granddaughter of John Mortlock I I I, (see *Mortlock of Cambridge Family Tree*), the founder of the first Bank of Cambridge, England, in 1780, and the Mayor of Cambridge from 1785 to 1810.

Frances' marriage connected the Griffiths family with the eminent and wealthy Mortlock family at a time of a serious family crisis. In 1843 Frances' cousin, John Frederick (J.F.) Mortlock (son of her uncle, Frederick Cheetham Mortlock), was convicted of a violent attack on his uncle, the Rev. Edmund Mortlock. John Frederick confronted Edmund Mortlock by holding a pistol to his head because he believed he had been defrauded of his rightful legacy by his uncles Edmund and Thomas after his father's death in 1838. Mortlock argued that he had only intended to frighten his uncle into an admission of fraud, and had only put a small amount of powder in the pistol so that it was harmless. This was borne out by the fact that when he fired the pistol, it had left only a small bruise on his uncle's face. Mortlock's accounting at his trial was noted by the editors G.A. Wilkes and A.G. Mitchell in a book Mortlock later wrote, *Experiences of a Convict*. Despite this defense, and an unsuccessful petition from the citizens of Cambridge on behalf of this popular young man, he was sentenced to be transported to Australia for twenty-one years.

Mortlock spent eighteen weeks in chains in the hulks at Portsmouth, and then four more months at sea before arriving at Port Jackson, Australia in January 1844. Although in the early years of his sentence he worked in detention with hard labor, he was not subjected to the worst of the penal system's brutalities thanks to his education and resourcefulness. During those years, he worked as a wardsman in a convict dormitory, watch-house keeper, schoolmaster, clerk, and storekeeper, and finally he obtained a license as a hawker. In 1864 he was finally declared a free man. During those years, he wrote eighteen pamphlets on various subjects, and also his memoir *Experiences of a Convict*, which now serves as a documentary record of Australian life from 1844 to 1864. Mortlock was described by those who knew him as a likable person with an engaging personality. On becoming a free man, he spent the rest of his life determined to get restitution of what he perceived as the wrongs committed against him by his uncles. He died June 21, 1882 never having achieved that goal.

My Connection to Indigenous Australia

Growing up in Australia, I was taught very little about the history of the indigenous people who had lived on the island continent I thought of as my home for at least 40,000 years before the arrival of Europeans. What little I knew of the Aboriginal culture in my youth nevertheless fascinated me. Even as a young child, I imagined how it must have been for them to live in harmony with each other and to be in intimate contact with a harsh land as hunters and food-gatherers. When I visited their most sacred place, Uluru in the Simpson Desert (renamed Ayers Rock by Europeans), and observed their cave paintings and carvings, I was acutely appreciative of the richness and beauty of their history and culture. Although they had no written language, the mythology of their Dreamtime was passed down from generation to generation through thousands of years to explain the mysteries of the universe. It was the inspiration for their art, music, and ceremonial life. Over the years, my progression from the formal religion I learned as a child to an inner sense of spirituality was influenced by my awareness of and admiration for the Aboriginal culture.

I have written this book in the hope that my children, my grandchildren, and their children's children will find their roots in this accounting of some of their ancestors. I hope that my voice will come to them through the ages, and that they will know how much I love the ones I already know, and the ones of the future that I wish I could know.

John Mortlock III, my Great-Great-Great Grandfather. banker, magistrate, mayor of Cambridge, and (briefly) member of Parliament. Father of Captain Charles Mortlock (below). (See Mortlock Family Tree, page 146)

JOHN MORTLOCK   1708–1775

Captain Charles Mortlock, my Great-Great Grandfather. Went to sea at age 12 in the Honourable East India Company's Maritime Service (HEICMS). He rose to be the senior commander in the HEICMS. This picture was taken at the time of his retirement to Brighton in 1860

Griffiths Family Military Service

Many members of my family, including my father, his brothers, cousins, and their male descendants, were military men. Some I briefly name here, and include in more detail at the end of this epilogue.

Theodore Ralph Houghton Griffiths, Major British Army; Aug 10,1886 – Dec 13,1964 – my father.

Noel Stewart Griffiths, Cdr Royal Navy, US L of Merit – October 18, 1896 – June 26, 1982, my father's brother. Awarded the US Legion of Merit for distinguished service during the planning and execution of the invasion of Normandy

Peter Eric Noel Griffiths, Cdr Royal Navy, DSC – July 24, 1920 – 2017 – son of Noel Grifffiths.

Robin Francis Houghton Griffiths, 2/Lt British Army – Sept 15,1914 – Aug 16,1938 – my father's first born son. Mortally wounded on August 16, 1938 by a land mine in Palestine.

John Stuart Griffiths – February 27, 1916 – Sept 6, 1945 – my father's second son. Pte Hampshire Regiment British Army – invalided 1937, and again 1940.

Robert Jeremy Houghton Griffiths, Lt Cdr Royal Navy – April 22, 1937 – Robin Griffiths' son.

Career of
Theodore Ralph Houghton Griffiths

2/Lt 4 Bn N Staffordshire Regt & others 25.9.1905-26.5.1908 (Militia)

2/Lt East Lancashire Regt 27.5.08-6.1911 at home & India
Mounted Infantry School 10.1909-2.1910
Lieutenant 16.6.1911

West India Regt 20.10.11-4.8.13

West Africa Regt 4.8.13-20.7.15 (sick 29.10.14, invalided, Black Water fever)

14 Bn Royal Scots 20.7.15-2.11.15

Indian Army (France) 2.11.15-8.3.16

O.C. 2 Rajput Light Infantry (Mesopotamia) 8.3.16-31.8.16
Captain 20.4.16 (Acting Captain 8.3.16); wounded 16.4.16,
& compulsorily transferred to Manchester Regt, invalided.

2 I/c Nelson Battalion, Royal Naval Division (France) 16.1.17-8.3.17 (sick
9.3.17, invalided)

1st(G) Worcester Regt 2.6.17-15.7.17

Adjutant 33 Territorial Bn then 51st Hampshire Regt 25.7.17-16.11.17

2 I/c 7th British West Indies Regt 1.12.17-23.5.19, T/Major 1.12.17-3.8.19
Recommended by CO 7 BWIR for Mention in Despatches in 1919 New Year
honours but it was not awarded

Senior Officers' School 1.4.1919-16.5.19

Depot (O.C.) BWIR 23.5.19-3.8.19

Major Griffiths, ca. 1914

War Office 3.8.19-31.10.19 (repatriation office & recruiting of volunteer officers for (failed) campaign of White Russian General Nicolai Yudenitch)

2nd Bn West India Regt (Jamaica) 11.2.20
Passed for Major 4.1921
Date of substantive promotion to Major unknown
Date of leaving army unknown

Robin and John

By Robert Griffiths

Houghton and Elsie had two children, Robin (born 15 September 1914) and John (27 February 1916). After Elsie separated from Houghton she obtained cut-price places for the boys at a preparatory school run by her mother's friend, and then presentations for both to Christ's Hospital. Robin was early a tearaway. Like his father he never wanted to be anything but a soldier, and on his eighteenth birthday took the train to London and enlisted. After two years in the ranks, during which he qualified as a physical training instructor, in 1934 he was one of only twelve Other Ranks given a King's Cadetship to Sandhurst. In 1936 he was commissioned into the Manchester Regiment, one of the few where an officer could live on his pay. Turning down an offer to be ADC (aide-de-camp) to the Duke of Connaught, he joined B company of the 1st Battalion, initially in Egypt. In April 1938 the battalion was ordered to Palestine to combat the Arab revolt. On 16 August Robin was riding in a lorry with troops escorting Jewish workmen, when it exploded an Arab land mine and he was mortally wounded. His mother was left the task of bringing up baby Robert, Robin's 15-month-old son by his wife Mary Bosanquet.

John was always a sickly child and after years of sinus surgery had to leave school at 14 to go to South Africa to escape the English winter, funding for which trip was provided by Queen Mary after Johndy's surgeon, who was also treating the future King George VI, told her of the case. Johndy had to give up a cabinet-making apprenticeship and then a job with a furniture painter, in both cases because of sinus trouble, and instead joined the Hampshire Regiment in 1936, from which he was invalided in 1937. He then set up and ran a roadside café in a converted bus. When the war started he shut up the café and went straight back to his regiment, but was invalided again in 1940. Fainting fits meant that he had to give up a job in de Havillands, and then as a Red Cross ambulance driver, and although he restarted his café in 1945 his body finally gave up on him and he died on 6 September.

Johndy, Houghton, and Robin Griffiths, 1918

Noel and Peter Griffiths

By Robert Griffiths

Talbot's youngest child, Noel Stewart Griffiths, was bullied at his first Public School, St John's Leatherhead, and was removed to Worksop College to complete his schooling. In 1913 he became a Special Entry Naval Cadet under a scheme started by Jackie Fisher, who realised that the Osborne and Dartmouth process would not produce enough Naval Officers to meet the threat from Germany, and that the numbers coming through from the 13-year-old entry to Osborne must be supplemented by Public School men brought in at 17 and 18. Noel was one of the very first of this entry.

After initial training Noel was appointed to the new battleship Warspite as a Midshipman. On leaving Warspite as an Acting Sub Lieutenant, Noel was appointed to a patrol boat at Milford Haven. Noel risked his career by taking leave to visit his wounded brother Eric, to whom he was particularly close. After serving on the battleship Benbow in the Mediterranean as a lieutenant, he was briefly among the Naval Officers sent up to Cambridge to finish their education which had been interrupted by the War. Noel then joined the Colonial Service in Nigeria.

Thereafter he did some cloak-and-dagger stuff for the Foreign Office in Turkey—in old age he could sometimes be tempted to show passports full of exotic endorsements. Reemployed by the Royal Navy in 1939, Noel, aged 47, was assigned to Combined Operations, and on D-Day at Omaha Beach, he was assigned to run a scheme where freighters would beach on the tide. His service gained him the U.S. Legion of Merit.

Noel's son, Peter Griffiths, also became a Special Entry Naval Cadet in 1939, and was also in the Normandy Invasion—perhaps a father-and-son record—where he was in the only HM Ship (HMS Wrestler, mined at 0645 when the party had hardly started) to be knocked out completely on D-Day. Wrestler was damaged beyond repair and was sold for scrap a few days later. In December 1941, as a newly-promoted Lieutenant, Peter had won a DSC as

Noel Griffiths
Legion of Merit

Admiral Henri Kent Hewitt
US Navy
Grosvenor Square
3rd June 1946

Legion of Merit

Uncle Noel award, 1946

Asdic Officer of HMS Blankney, a Hunt-class destroyer, which helped sink two U-boats on a particularly fraught Gibraltar convoy. Blankney's CO, Lt Cdr Powlett, received a well-deserved DSO for these U-boat sinkings and there were other awards. Peter's DSC citation recalled how he had controlled the ship's Asdics most skillfully on both occasions, implying that it was his professional skill that had caused the critical damage to the enemy which brought each U-boat to the surface so that it could be sunk by the subsequent gunfire.

After the war Peter specialised formally in Torpedoes and Anti-Submarine Warfare and was sent to San Diego on exchange with the United States Navy. Hardly had he settled Sue and their three children (Noel, Jane and Sally) in California than he was told he had been promoted to Commander in the half-yearly list.

ref: PRO ADM1/12261, Honours and Awards to HM Ships Exmoor and Blankney December 1941 etc.

Career of Robert Jeremy Houghton Griffiths

1954 Passed into the Royal Navy top of the last 17-18 year old officer entry.

1955 One term at Dartmouth (top of final exams), two cruises in cadet training aircraft carrier HMS Triumph, to Scandinavia, Leningrad and the Mediterranean. First Class pass on completion.

1956 Midshipman, submarine depot ship HMS Maidstone four months, then ten months in Far East in cruiser HMS Newfoundland which included Suez deployment to Red Sea where Newfoundland sank the Egyptian frigate Domiat. First Class pass in Midshipman's Board.

1957 Acting Sub Lieutenant, destroyer HMS Cossack at Singapore.

1957-8 Two terms at Royal Naval College Greenwich. Staff training and Humanities.

1958-9 Technical courses around Portsmouth, First Class passes in all.

1959-60 Sub Lieutenant and then Lieutenant (with maximum seniority gain), HMS Tiger (new cruiser). Baltic and the Mediterranean Fleet Flagship.

1960-62 First Lieutenant HMS Highburton and, later, Clarbeston (minesweepers) employed at Portland on trials of experimental equipment.

1962-3 Long Gunnery Course. First Class pass.

1963-5 New Guided Missile Destroyer, HMS London, South America and Far East. Involved in Indonesian Confrontation including service in Tawau (Borneo) guard ship HMS Loch Fada.

1965-6 Advanced Gunnery Course, RN College Greenwich (intensive maths, science and computing course).

1966-8 HMS Euryalus as Lieutenant Commander (first of term to achieve that rank and, on promotion, the youngest Lt Cdr in the RN) and Squadron Gunnery Officer, 1st Frigate Squadron. Scandinavia, US, Canada and Far East (circumnavigation via Cape of Good Hope and Panama). Landed for internal security for independence of Mauritius.

1968-71 Gunnery Action Data Automation Rule Writer, Admiralty Surface Weapons Establishment Portsmouth, mostly on 'Seawolf' embryonic guided missile system.

1971-1993 Various always different and usually fascinating jobs with IBM UK near Portsmouth. Instant expert in, successively, stock control, financial systems, Information Security, Mini/Micro manufacturing applications, IT plans and controls, Artificial Intelligence and Electronic Data Interchange. Lots of travel on expenses. Closed this career with an aerial circumnavigation via Australia and the US.

1993- present Gentleman of Leisure courtesy of IBM's pension roll.

William, Robert, and Harry Griffiths, 2018

Family Tree Charts

The following pages contain charts of the Mortlock and Griffiths family trees. Dates use the British style of Day.Month.Year.

𝕸ortlock of 𝕮ambridge

John MORTLOCK III ======= Elizabeth Mary
17.10.55E-7.5.16E*   3.10.1776M   1756-5.4.17E*

- Stephen
  28.12.78M
  -29.8.79M

- Thomas@
  27.1.80M
  25.4.59GtA*
  lawyer&
  banker
  - Sir
    John
    Cheetham
    12.8.77K-
    3.11.45MB
    Eton&
    Queens,
    Middle
    Temple
    kt1816
  - Charles
    21.10.82E-
    24.10.64

- Frederick
  Cheetham
  3.8.1785
  -1838
  Eton,
  P'house&
  St Johns
  8thWranglr
  MdlTemple,
  LinclnsInn
  unm.

- Edmund
  Davy@'
  18.1.87E
  30.5.73*
  Moulton Sfk
  BStE grmr
  &Christ's
  14Wranglr
  unm.

- William
  27.5.91-
  22.6.48E*
  unm.
  alderman
  - Henry@
    16.7.89E
    V
    V
    3 daus

- Eliza'
  15.5.81M
  -1865
  =18.7.15GtA
  John
  KAYE DD FRS
  1783-1853
  bishop of
  Lincoln
  - Mary Anne
    11.7.92E-
    5.6.53*
    Moulton unm.
  - William Frederick John
    archdeacon of Lincoln

```
        Capt James THOMAS ======= Ann Elizabeth WOODHOUSE
        1747-18.1.31*#          | 12.11.1761
        S.Luffenham Rutland     |
                                |
                         V
                         V
    Charles 27.4.1809N
    MORTLOCK ========= Emelia Ann Elizabeth === Henry
    21.10.82E-         13.9.88N-                MORTLOCK
    24.10.64           30.10.73                 |
    Brighton           Brighton      issue
    capt.HEICMS

  Ann        Amelia     Frances'   Charles  Mary'    Charles@  John         Edward
  Elizabeth  7.5.11~    13.10.15G  26.8.17G Ann      23.1.21C  16.11.23P    Thomas@
  26.1.10N-  bp7.6.11G  -28.8.66   d.inf    31.3.19G           -17.4.45     6.8.26P-
  >1881      -17.4.45   =                    -2Q79             Dharwar      24.5.08
  =2.10.45   Salem      Rev. John           =23.10.37          India
  TamilNadu  Madras     GRIFFITHS           |Marylebone        Lt35MNI
  Alexander Wm                              |(lic.)            cholera
  Phillips HEICS                            |Rev.W BLYTH
  1819-25.2.83Southsea                      10s/d

Caroline 11.5.13G-<1868
         V       6.1807
         X

                                        @=cf Alumni Cantabriensis
```

```
              V
              X          6.1807
       Frederick Cheetham  ======  Sarah FINCH
       1784-22.8.38          Gretna & 3.12.88- 28.3.1884 GtE*(+at LtA)
       bur.Chelsea           (& Melford 25.7.07(separated 1830))

 |              |            |           |          |             |
John       Frederick    William      Emily      Catherine    Elizabeth
Frederick  William      5.7.19E-     1811/?7-44 Frances      Sarah
8.8.09E-   1813         9.7.1864     bur.Westley 1816-18.3.86# 1808/9-
21.6.82                 17.3.17E-    =10.8.39LT  =22.7.37LT    4.1.99 as
Strand RD,              29.3.05      Rev.Thos    Rev.Chas W    MORTLOCK
London     Rev.         Abington     HALSTEAD    LAMPRELL
transported Charles     dragoon      +4.1.99     +1866
1843                    bur.GtE*                 Stradishall
                        unm/dsp

                    Mary (Maggy)                          dau
                    1822-4.2.29*<-- Aldeburgh -->d.inf


B=StBene't      E=StEdward       M=StMary Gt all Cambridge      P=Pampisford
C=H Trinity Clapham Sy   G=St George Southwark   N=St Mary Newington Southwark
GtA=Great Abington       GtE=Great Eversden      LtE=Little Eversden
MB=Marylebone London     LT=Little Thurlow
```

for further detail, both of other descendants and of the Mortlock ancestry going
back in Pampisford, Cambs, to the Wars of the Roses, see also
http://www.mortlock.info/mortlock-encyclopedia.html (the Bankers)

Griffiths Tree

```
                                              25.1.1844                            26.10.1868
Frances MORTLOCK        ========== (1) Rev.John GRIFFITHS (2) ==========    Caroline
13.10.15 Southwark-     Brighton       <15.9.1813-              Calicut     Lydia BAKER
28.8.66 Cuddalore                      13.10.91 Tunbridge Wells             23.1.1833
"of apoplexy"                          Christ Church, Oxford                Hamburg-
                                       Senior Chaplain, Madras              2.7.1895 T.Wells
                                       chaplain to Earl Brownlow, Belton Hall
                                       Anglican chaplain, La Spezia
                    |-----------------------------------------------------------|
       20.10.1884
Mabel  ========== Rev.Talbot Monckton Milnes         Emily      Frances Emma Jane
Ida    Calcutta   6.11.55 Waltair-                    1845-7     23.8.46 Mangalore-
ANDERSON          13.11.29 London                                <12.7.1935 Poole
                  Ipswich School & Keble, Oxford                 =11.8.1868
                  rector Warmingham Cheshire                     Calicut
                  chaplain to the Marquess of Crewe              Major General
                  (his cousin)                                   Arthur Matcham DAVIES
```

```
Theodore              Vera                 Beryl                 Charles   Eric-John
Ralph                 Gwendolyn            Frances               Groyn     Mortlock
Houghton              Leila                10.5.1890Kasauli-|    1895      4.6.1892
Major WIR    13.2.1889Sitapur-    1976Papakura               d.inf     Mussoorie-
10.8.1886Cuttack-  1975Papakura                                          14.2.1975
13.12.64Adelaide  =30.7.1918Bedwelty(div.) V                             Salisbury
(1)=27.11.1913   John'that rat'LIMNER    +2.pp                           S.Rhodesia
|Alverstoke
|Elsie C BURRIDGE1886-1976            Rupert                          V    Noel
                                     Hildebrand                      +4.pp Stewart
                                     Lt Col MC CdeG                        Cdr RN
                                     10.6.1891                       US L of Merit
Robin Francis Houghton  John Stuart  Kasauli-                        18.10.1896
15.9.1914Gosport-    27.2.1916-      12.2.1981                       Landour-
16.8.38          6.9.1945Haslemere s.p.  Hurlingham                  26.6.1982
2/Lt Manchester Regt                                                 Orleans
kia Palestine                                      V                      V
=(1)                                              +3.pp                   +5.pp

| Florence Mary Theodora BOSANQUET   (2)=2.8.1940Liskeard,HGS SAUNDERS
| 21.12.1912Malvern-17.10.2000Farnham           Major RM 1915-2003

Robert Jeremy Houghton            Richard Bosanquet Scott     Timothy Cosmo Scott
22.4.1937Clearwell, Glos          22.5.1943Cearwell-          16.3.1948Southwold
=24.9.1966RNC Greenwich           17.6.1960Durdle Door
|Ann Stilwell FREELAND
|23.3.1939Stanmore Mx
```

Rupert Freeland Houghton   Dr William James Houghton ====== Mellisa Sue
14.2.1968Plymouth-   FRCP PhD Ipswich MEDFORD
5.4.2000Portsmouth   10.2.1970Emsworth   1994

Harry Medford
14.3.1999Cambridge

previous page
V
28.7.1931
Theodore Ralph Houghton(2) ======= Vera Ellen Charlotte JUSTICE
Adelaide   3.12.1908Adelaide-4.3.1986Adelaide

Jillian Vera
12.3.1936
=
Dr Jack HUSSEY

Mary Ouida
2.6.1934-
12.3.1986

Adam William
ANDERSON
27.5.1963

David John Milnes
26.9.1932Quambi SA-
1.4.2017Alwyndor SA
=
Peggy Louise
b.Bristol

151

Matthew David
7.11.1964
=8.5.1991
|Robin VANCE
|

Dr Stephen Bourne
12.5.1967
=8.9.2004
|Gisela SOBOLL
|DVM MS PhD
|

Katherine Anne
17.1.1969
=6.9.1992
|Todd YOUNG
|

Reese Stephen
8.5.1993

Savannah Rae
24.7.1997

Alexander John
27.2.1997

Erik
Edward
29.9.99

Rebecca
Katherine
17.1.2002

Benjamin Bourne
20.6.2004

Anja Isabella
18.3.2006

Susan Louise
31.3.1957
(1)= div.

Paul David Milnes
6.10.1959
= (div.)
|Joanne MARCIC
|

Bronwyn Elizabeth
31.4.1961-1989

Deborah Jane
22.3.1963
~
|Stuart
|CUNNINGHAM
|

(2)=

Erwald
ZAUCHENBERGER
b.Austria

Aaron

Elijah

Tara

Declan
8.3.1992

```
                    -2.pp
                      V        13.8.1915
              Beryl Frances ======= Lewis (Taff) DAVIES
                             Conway RD 1891->1968Papakura
                                       Wales
```

Stewart Mortlock Robert (Tony) 4.4.1916 Wem (Salop) - 4.11.2002 Papakura =

Eric Francis 1918-17.4.1941 kia Greece b.Phaleron

Alec

Rupert

Bettine 15.12.1925Auckland- 12.8.1995 Garden Grove CA USA =5.7.1944 |Auckland |John Louis KENNA |3.12.1923Iowa- |1.12.1997 |Garden Grove |Orange CA

Kerry   Steven

(1)Dawn
  (2)=
      CAIN

Michael   Karen   Chris   Linda

Anthony 1950   Ken   Yvonne   Eric   Gaylene

```
Eric J          Katherine     Timothy J      Maureen        Michael P   Kerry         Mary
8.4.1945        Ellen         28.9.1954      Anne           1957        Patrick       Teresa
Auckland        2.11.1952     Charleston     5.1.1956       V           23.1.1958     1960
=23.9.72        Gt Lakes Ill  NC             Bethesda MD    V           L.Angeles     =
|Cherrie        =19.9.1970                   =2.7.1977                  =             |Daniel L
|Sue            |Lavon L                     |Orange CA                 |GOLDSBERRY   |STRINGHAM
|CONNELLY       |SMITH                       |John H                    |
|27.10.45                                    |GIFFORD                   1s.1d
|
1s.            Melody
               =TAYLOR
                                        Daniel James  1d
                                        23.7.1980


               Michelle Clarisse    Kelly Lynn        Melissa Sue
               27.11.84Anaheim CA   4.11.87           6.2.93
               ~                    S Juan Capistrano CA   Garden Grove
               Justin Ray ALDIS                            13.3.2015=
               1989                                        Fullerton CA
                                                           Landon Spencer
                                                           JERNIGAN

VRJHG
V     23.10.1981
Michael P ======= Barbara A ORTIZ
          Bexar TX
```

Michael ====== Tina Sue BUTLER
18.10.2003
Nevada

Alan Julyan ======(2)Evelina Esther(1)========= Rupert Hildebrand
DONKIN Calcutta ('Cissie') MADDISON Marylebone
Lt Col RA   15.5.1897-27.11.1989
18.9.1941   9.9.1918   -3.pp
                                          V

George BLAKE ======= Celia Noreen
Major RM Hayling I 12.4.1919Emsworth-4.11.1994Hayling I
14.8.1941

Patricia Jane
26.3.1942Surrey SW
=12.10.1963Hayling I
|Air Cdre John DELAFIELD

Carol A
10.1943Marylebone
=4.1968Westminster
|Sq Ldr Geoffrey JONES RAF
3s

Charles
6.1948-1994Portsmouth
=
Jeanette

Judy Margaret
4.9.1965Louth
=1.10.1999Noke, Oxon
Michael J C JILLINGS

Richard John
17.1.1968N Kesteven Lincs
=5.9.1998Hyby, Sweden
Maria WILLFORD-PERRSON

```
                        3Q1935
Walter Daniel STARR ========= Rose Maud FUTTER ~ Rupert Hildebrand
2.2.1907Ferndale- Biggleswade    25.10.1914
1Q1993Bexhill                    Biggleswade-
                                 3Q2002Bexhill

            Marian E
          2Q1937Hitchin
4Q1977Waltham Forest=(1)
     Brian J TURNER|
        artist|
           ?

        ?=(2)

     2Q1958          1Q1976
Roy D ======(1)Barbara(2)======(1)Christopher Rupert
JARMAINE Bromley  BONSTEAD  Bromley  9.1945Hitchin

                    Virginia Arabella
                      3Q1977Dover

                                  2010
                        (2)=========Susan CLARK
                           Chelsea O.Ch
```

```
                          -4.pp
                            v
                        15.6.1920
Joan ECCLES ========(1) Eric-John Mortlock(2) ======== Betty BYROM STYLE
            WestKirby                                   5.4.1905-
            Cheshire                                    4.4.1994'Harare'


Joan Margery        Ethel Marion
14.7.1921WKirby-    5.1.1925Runcorn
12.1988Chichester
unm.
                    =?1968,Barry LYNDON (div.)
                    =6.1970Hastings
                    Robert PATERSON +?1986Malta
                    =1988,Baron Van WEESEL+~1997


Jennifer Jane       John Grahame Mortlock   Richard Mortlock    Peter James Mortlock
15.7.1934Bulowayo   15.3.1937S.Rhodesia     3.5.1938Salisbury   30.1.1941Salisbury
=                   (1)=                     =
|Paul Randolph      |Ann WRIGHT             |Phyllis Margaret    |Jenny
|Eden TITTERTON     |                       |HARPER              =
|div.1998         he|
|      ?2018=(2)|                                                David Asher
|         Gail                                                   15.7.1975
|      FITZGERLD
```

```
                                                              Zane John
                                         Lance Barry Mortlock  24.10.1971
                                         27.5.1965Salisbury
                  Kevin Richard
                  17.3.1961
                  =
                  |Jane Hazel MARTIN
                                         Kristopher Dean  Ashlee Cassandra
                                         1992             1995
                                                                Scott Deon
                                                                1975
                                                                =
                                                                |Kt Gail
         George TYLER
she                         Marc Grahame Mortlock
(2)=1.1999                  22.8.1971Salisbury

                  Tracey Lee
                  1965
                  =
                  |Johnny HALE
                                    Tamsin Louise  Megan Alaxandra  George
```

```
Diana Karen Eden        Cheryl Ann Eden      Paula
9.11.1957Bulowayo-      9.6.1960Bulowayo     4.2.1975
13.10.1972              =                    changed sex to Alix WELSH
                        STARK                =(2)Kerry Lyn WELSH(1)=Stephen RICE
                        (div.<2001

                        ?~'Rob'              Harlon Lindsay      Madison Shannon
                                             28.12.1994Sydney    28.12.1994-6.6.2016Skye


                                 -5.pp
                                  V                1931
Olga Vavasour JONAS =======(1)Noel Stewart(2)===== Molly BLACKBURN
                        Cambridge              Batley
                                                       1959
                        Peter Eric Noel           Patricia ==== Roland
             24.7.1920-2017Okehampton      13.10.193Hove ROBITAILLIE
                        Cdr RN DSC
                           V
                        next page
```

```
Carolyn              Elizabeth              Sophie
29.3.1961Hove        1.9.1963Hove           14.10.1965Hove
=3.6.1984            =21.11.1987            =20.9.1986Combleux
|Jean-Louis RAMON    |Pierre Francois       |Dr Régis FERNAGU
|(anaesthetist)      |GERBAUD               |(GP)
|1950-               |(div.2005)
|8.2018              |(urologist)


        Adélaïde       Victoire    Géraldine   Clothilde   Mahault
        7.9.1990       8.9.1987    14.2.1990   17.1.1994   25.10.1996
        =8.2014        =6.2018
        Quentin DENYS  |Aymeric
                       |GUILLAUME-DUVERNE
                       |Octave
                       |3.6.2019

                       Sybil          Leonor        Sarah
                       14.11.1991     20.4.1995     17.2.1997
                                      =?2020
                                      Alexandre
```

```
Marie-Andre     Diane        Ann Laure
29.11.1984      20.4.1987    1.12.1987    }all Orleans
=
|Charles-Antoine
|FOURNEL

Victoire     Castille
20.4.2014    9.4.2019

previous page
      V
Peter Eric Noel ====== Suzanne V E GAIN
6.7.1946
Chatham  30.8.1924-14.7.2012

                              1980
              Sarah Ann (Sallie)==== Richard
                    1953            BUSTON

              Sarah MSc         Nicola Jane
              5.1880            14.4.1992
                                =
                                |SINGER
```

Alicia   1s   Sam Elliott   1d
5.2011   23.12.2010

29.2.1980
Noel ======== Ann

Toby Oliver ========== 22.8.2009 Lauran
14.1.1983 Dunfermline BRIDGEHOUSE
Staff Sgt RAMC

Charlotte Anne
23.3.2013

Bryan CUNNINGHAM ======(2) Jane(1) = Graham WEBSTER
6.2004   1947

Ross Murray ===== Helen

Ellie Jane   Harry
2001

Sarah ===== Piers
8.2000   Seaford

Ross Benjamin   Piers   Amberlily
1999   2001   2008

Jillian Hussey was born in Adelaide,
South Australia in 1936.
She spent the first twenty-five years
of her life living by the sea.

In 1957, she graduated as a registered nurse.
From 1961 to 1963,
under the sponsorship of the
American Nurses' Association (ANA),
she worked at Johns Hopkins Hospital in Baltimore,
followed by Colorado General Hospital in Denver.
At the end of her two-year contract with ANA,
instead of returning to Australia,
she made a decision to live in the United States
and married John Hussey.
She was naturalized as a U.S. citizen in 1972
For the past 58 years.
Jillian has returned every three years or so
to visit Australia, on two occasions
for a year at a time.
She has grown to love her
adopted country passionately,
but never stops missing the beloved
country of her birth.

If you would like to purchase a copy of this book,
visit Amazon.com and search for *Jill's Story: Between
Two Worlds* in Books.

Jillian Hussey was born in Adelaide,
South Australia in 1936.
She spent the first twenty-five years
of her life living by the sea.

In 1957, she graduated as a registered nurse.
From 1961 to 1963,
under the sponsorship of the
American Nurses' Association (ANA),
she worked at Johns Hopkins Hospital in Baltimore,
followed by Colorado General Hospital in Denver.
At the end of her two-year contract with ANA,
instead of returning to Australia,
she made a decision to live in the United States
and married John Hussey.
She was naturalized as a U.S. citizen in 1972
For the past 58 years.
Jillian has returned every three years or so
to visit Australia, on two occasions
for a year at a time.
She has grown to love her
adopted country passionately,
but never stops missing the beloved
country of her birth.

If you would like to purchase a copy of this book, visit Amazon.com and search for *Jill's Story: Between Two Worlds* in Books.

www.ingramcontent.com/pod-product-compliance
Lightning Source LLC
Chambersburg PA
CBHW041012140426

R18136400001B/R181364PG42813CBX00007B/3

9 7 8 1 9 4 5 5 7 5 0 1 3